T0386409

'*The Study of Words* is an excellent introduction to the field of Morphology. Specifically designed for students with little or no background in linguistics, it is clear and concise in its prose while providing a wide array of examples from a diverse range of languages.'

**John Boyle**, *California State University, Fresno, USA*

'Using a wide array of examples from English and diverse languages around the world, Professor Gebhardt lures the reader into an understanding of major principles of morphology as related to other areas of linguistics. Recommended as an introductory textbook or general resource.'

**Fred E. Anderson**, *Professor Emeritus, Kansai University, Japan*

# The Study of Words

*The Study of Words* introduces the study of word structure, also known as morphology, without assuming any prior knowledge of linguistics. Introducing concepts in an accessible way, Gebhardt illustrates how to understand and produce both existing and new words. This book:

- Provides an overview of words, word components and the rules by which components can and cannot be assembled into words;
- Introduces the area of morphology with a data-driven approach, exposing readers to sets of words in a variety of languages and prompting them to identify their components and seek patterns;
- Features exercises and questions throughout to provoke thought and point readers to unresolved morphological issues.

Aimed at students at undergraduate level with no background in linguistics, *The Study of Words* is essential reading for those studying morphology for the first time as part of linguistics, language and general education courses.

**Lewis Gebhardt** is Associate Professor of Linguistics at Northeastern Illinois University, Chicago, USA. As well as teaching morphology for the past decade, his main research interests are syntax, morphology and semantics.

# Routledge Guides to Linguistics

Series Editor: Betty J. Birner is a Professor of Linguistics and Cognitive Science in the Department of English at Northern Illinois University.

*Routledge Guides to Linguistics* are a set of concise and accessible guidebooks which provide an overview of the fundamental principles of a subject area in a jargon-free and undaunting format. Designed for students of Linguistics who are approaching a particular topic for the first time, or students who are considering studying linguistics and are eager to find out more about it, these books will both introduce the essentials of a subject and provide an ideal springboard for further study.

This series is published in conjunction with the Linguistic Society of America. Founded in 1924 to advance the scientific study of language, the LSA plays a critical role in supporting and disseminating linguistic scholarship both to professional linguists and to the general public.

**Titles in this series:**

**Language in African American Communities**
*Sonja Lanehart*

**The Study of Words**
An Introduction
*Lewis Gebhardt*

More information about this series can be found at https://www.routledge.com/Routledge-Guides-to-Linguistics/book-series/RGL

Linguistic Society of America

# The Study of Words

An Introduction

Lewis Gebhardt

Routledge
Taylor & Francis Group

LONDON AND NEW YORK

First published 2023
by Routledge
4 Park Square, Milton Park, Abingdon, Oxon OX14 4RN

and by Routledge
605 Third Avenue, New York, NY 10158

*Routledge is an imprint of the Taylor & Francis Group, an informa business*

*British Library Cataloguing-in-Publication Data*
A catalogue record for this book is available from the British Library

*Library of Congress Cataloging-in-Publication Data*
Names: Gebhardt, Lewis, author.
Title: The study of words: an introduction/Lewis Gebhardt.
Description: Abingdon, Oxon; New York, NY: Routledge, 2023. |
Series: Routledge guides to linguistics | Includes bibliographical references and index.
Identifiers: LCCN 2022044226 (print) | LCCN 2022044227 (ebook) |
ISBN 9780367466435 (hardback) | ISBN 9780367466411 (paperback) |
ISBN 9781003030188 (ebook)
Subjects: LCSH: Grammar, Comparative and general–Morphology.
Classification: LCC P241.G43 2023 (print) | LCC P241 (ebook) |
DDC 415/.9–dc23/eng/20221004
LC record available at https://lccn.loc.gov/2022044226
LC ebook record available at https://lccn.loc.gov/2022044227

ISBN: 978-0-367-46643-5 (hbk)
ISBN: 978-0-367-46641-1 (pbk)
ISBN: 978-1-003-03018-8 (ebk)

DOI: 10.4324/9781003030188

Typeset in Times New Roman
by Deanta Global Publishing Services, Chennai, India

This book is dedicated to my Master's morphology students, to most of whose questions I can best answer, "That would make a great thesis topic!"

# Contents

# Acknowledgments

Many thanks to Shahrzad Mahootian, Judy Kaplan-Weinger and Fred Anderson for their vital input on the text. Also, thanks to the Routledge editors and their very generous patience, especially to Betty Birner for her support and comments.

# List of Abbreviations

| | |
|---|---|
| * | an ungrammatical expression |
| * | a reconstructed form of an expression in an earlier stage of the language |
| 1 | first person |
| 2 | second person |
| 3 | third person |
| A | adjective |
| ACC | accusative |
| ACT | active voice |
| AOR | aorist |
| CAUSE | causative |
| CM | class marker |
| DAT | dative |
| DECL | declarative |
| DEF | definite |
| DET | determiner |
| DO | direct object |
| DU | dual number |
| FEM | feminine |
| FUT | future |
| HAB | habitual |
| IMMPAST | immediate past |
| IMP | imperative |
| INDIC | indicative mood |

| | |
|---|---|
| IO | indirect object |
| MASC | masculine |
| N | noun |
| NEG | negative |
| NOM | nominative |
| P | preposition |
| PASS | passive |
| PAST | past tense |
| PASTP | past participle |
| PERF | perfect aspect |
| PERFP | perfect participle |
| PL | plural number |
| POT | potential |
| PRES | present tense |
| Q | question marker |
| SG | singular number |
| SUBJ | subject |
| V | verb |

# Glossary of Terms

**abbrevation** – Generally, the shortening of expressions into new words. Specifically, the creation of words based on spelling that are read as letter sequences. Taking the initial letters from *Federal Bureau of Investigation* yields *FBI*, with each of the letters pronounced individually.

**ablaut** – Inflection by altering the vowel of the stem. *Goose* has an ablaut plural of *geese*.

**accusative** – A case marking usually indicating the direct object of the verb. The pronoun form *him* is the English accusative masculine pronoun, as in *the dog bit him*.

**acronym** – A kind of lexeme formation that typically takes the first letter of each of the words in an expression to spell a new word. *UNESCO* is an acronym for *United Nations Educational, Scientific and Cultural Organization*.

**active** – A so-called voice, a form of the verb used when, stated simply, the subject of the verb is also the doer or experiencer of the verb. Most of the time, most verbs are used in the active voice. *Dickens wrote long novels; the kitty is sleeping;* and *did they buy the books?* are all sentences with active verbs. See **passive**.

**adjective** – A word category typically functioning to modify nouns. In both *a tall woman entered the room* and *the woman is tall*, the word *tall* is an adjective.

**adposition** – A word category including both prepositions and postpositions.

**affix** – A bound morpheme, excluding bound roots, that is added to a stem. There are many kinds of affixes for number on nouns, tense and agreement on verbs, etc. See **prefix**, **suffix**, **circumfix** and **infix**.

**agglutinating** – An agglutinating language can form long words by stringing together a series of affixes, each with a unique and dedicated function or meaning. For example, one suffix may indicate person, another tense and yet another to show whether a verb is a statement or a question.

**agreement** – A relationship between elements in a sentence whereby features of one element are reflected morphologically on the other. In *Anna thinks quinoa is overrated*, the word *thinks*, with the *-s* suffix for third-person singular, agrees with the third-person singular subject *Anna*.

**allomorph** – Allomorphs are variant pronunciations of a morpheme. The negative prefix *in-* ('not') has at least three allomorphs: [ɪn] in *inoperable*, [ɪm] in *impossible* and [ɪŋ] in *incoherent*. Less obviously, *in-* pops up in *illiterate* and *irreparable*.

**argument** – A constituent called for by a word, usually the verb. The verb *sleep* has one argument: the subject who sleeps. *Eat* has two arguments: the subject who eats and the object that gets eaten. The verb *give* typically has three arguments: a giver subject, the direct object being given and the indirect object that the direct object is given to.

**aspect** – A grammatical category reflecting characteristics of a verb such as whether the action is completed, durational or instantaneous, etc. In the expression *We are singing*, the *are* form of the verb *be*, along with the *-ing* form of the verb, indicates progressive aspect, implying duration of the singing event.

**auxiliary** – A so-called helping verb that accompanies a verbal participle to make certain tense, aspect and other forms. The auxiliary *have* appears in the form *we have arrived*. Other auxiliaries include *be* for passives, as in *she was elected mayor*, and *do*, often used in questions such as *did you find your keys?*.

**backformation** – A wordformation process that removes a supposed affix to create a new word, usually of another category. The noun *edit* was backformed from *editor*.

**base** – A root serving as the start of wordformation. In the word *word-formation*, the root $\sqrt{\text{FORM}}$ is accessed in the lexicon and then used as a base for adding morphemes. A base is the minimal case of a stem.

**blend** – A usually conscious kind of wordformation that takes pieces of two or more words and unites them into a new word. A good example of a blend is *smog*, from *smoke* and *fog*.

**borrowing** – The transfer of morphemes, usually whole words, from other languages. The preceding sentence has four words based on foreign sources: *transfer*, *morpheme*, *usual* (with the English suffix *-ly* added on) and *language*.

**bound morpheme** – A morpheme that never appears alone but must be attached to something – plural *-s* is a bound morpheme, as is past tense *-ed*. See **free morpheme**.

**case** – Morphological case is the inflectional expression of the function of nouns in a sentence. The feminine pronoun *she* is nominative case, typically used for the subject of a sentence: *she likes Russian short stories*. The *her* form is accusative case when the pronoun is the object of a sentence: *we saw her*.

**category** – A class or kind of morpheme based on meaning and behavior. Commonly recognized categories are verbs, nouns and adjectives. Verbs typically express events or states of affairs. In terms of behavior, English verbs have subjects, sometimes objects, and have tense in main clauses.

**circumfix** – An affix that appears in two pieces simultaneously with a prefixal portion and a suffixed portion. The participle of the German verb *machen* ('to make') is *ge-mach-t*, with the circumfix *ge ... t* appearing on both sides of the stem *mach*.

**clitic** – A phonetically weakened form of a word that is necessarily attached to another word and doesn't itself receive any stress. Some so-called English contractions are clitics, such as future *'ll* for *will* and *n't* for *not*. In some languages, pronouns have cliticized weak forms.

**cognate** – Morphemes that are similar in sound and/or meaning in different languages and trace from the same ancestral root. The English word *bread*, the German word *Brot* and the Dutch word *brood*, all mean 'bread' and all descended from the same word in an early Germanic mother language. More abstractly, the English word *mother* and the Persian word *madær* are cognates, both meaning 'mother' and both from a common ancestor language spoken thousands of years ago.

**coinage** – The creation of words, often whimsically, but sometimes involving morphology. Coinage is usually an intentional process to create words with a certain flavor appropriate for a product to be marketed. *Teflon*, originally a trade name, is a good example of a coined word. *Tefl-* is semantically mysterious, though it may be a sort of superclipping of *polytetrafluoroethylene*, while the *-on* might be a suffix to impart a scientific nuance.

**comparative** – A form of an adjective expressing 'more, to a greater degree'. In English, the comparative of short adjectives is formed with the suffix *-er*, as in *greener*; longer adjectives use the independent word *more* before the adjective, as in *more interesting*.

**comparative linguistics** – The branch of linguistics that seeks patterns in similar languages with a goal of deciding whether some group of languages come from a common source or mother language. Comparative linguistics is an important tool in historical linguistics.

**complex word** – A word made up of at least two morphemes, such as *books*, *rollout*, *Catholicism*, *interventionist* and *bluebird*.

**compositional** – A word or phrase is semantically compositional if its meaning can be arrived at through the meanings of the parts and the rules for putting them together. The verb *walked* is compositional, from the basic verb *walk* and the *-ed* past tense marker, i.e., 'walk in the past'. *Doghouse* is quasicompositional. It is a kind of house that has something to do with dogs, and experience suggests that it means 'house that a dog lives in'. But on analogy with *gingerbread house* it could conceivably mean 'a house made out of dogs'. *Dogwood* isn't compositional. It's a tree more than just wood, and what it has to do with dogs is completely mysterious.

**compound** – A word formed by combining root lexemes. Examples are *bluebird*, *black hole*, *childproof*, *freeze-dry* and *sugar-free*.

**concatenate** – To arrange in a linear sequence. The segments in *cat* concatenate in a linear consonant-vowel-consonant arrangement. The plural *-s* concatenates on the right of *cat* to form the plural.

**coordinate compound** – In contrast to many modifier-head compounds involving a kind-of semantic interpretation, in coordinate compounds the parts are more semantically balanced. A producer-director is not so much a kind of director but someone who both produces and directs.

**cran morpheme** – A bound morpheme that appears in a single word. The terminology is based on the word *cranberry*, the only word that *cran-* originally appeared in, although the morpheme *cran-* has since been extended to form words such as *cranapple*, *cran raspberry*, *cran·mango*, etc.

**derivational morpheme** – A morpheme that derives one lexeme from another. The suffix *-ize* is a derivational morpheme, converting the adjective *national* into the verb *nationalize*.

**derivational morphology** – That part of the morphological system that produces new lexemes. The noun *education* derives from the verb *educate* via the derivational suffix *-tion*. In turn, the adjective *educational* is derived from the noun *education* via the derivational suffix *-al*.

**descriptive grammar** – An account of a language based on observing what speakers naturally do in conversation. A descriptivist observes that people do sometimes say *ain't* and do often end sentences with prepositions. See **prescriptive grammar**.

**dual** – Number morphology to indicate two of something, in contrast to other kinds of plural. In Lavukaleve, *mulukita-ul* means 'two oranges' while *mulukita-vil* means 'more than two oranges'.

**endocentric** – A compound is endocentric if the head of the compound is included in the compound. *Hamburger bun* is endocentric because the head, *bun*, is part of the compound; a hamburger bun is a kind of bun.

**evidential** – A morpheme expressing the speaker's assessment of the reliability of the information in an utterance. In Tuaca, the suffix *-wi* implies that the speaker personally observed a situation, while *-yigi* suggests that the speaker is reporting secondhand information.

**exclusive** – A first-person plural form, particularly in pronouns, that excludes the hearer. See **inclusive.**

**exocentric** – A compound is exocentric if the semantic head of the compound is not part of the compound. *Paperback* is exocentric because the understood semantic head, *book*, is not in the compound. A paperback is a kind of book, not a kind of back.

**feature** – Features are bits of information contained in a morpheme that specify meaning, sound and how the morpheme combines with other morphemes. Plural *-s* in English contains, among other things, a feature that specifies it must suffix to a noun. The English article *a* can be described as having the features [Determiner:Article:Indefinite; Singular; Used with count nouns].

**formative** – A morpheme-like unit in a word that has, at best, a vague semantic contribution but that is also recognizable in a number of words. The formative *-ceive* appears in *deceive*, *perceive*, *receive* and *conceive*. The prefixes *de-*, *per-*, *re-* and *con-*, also having no contribution to the semantics of the words, are formatives as well.

**free morpheme** – A morpheme that is a word by itself. In the preceding sentence, *a*, *that*, *is*, *word* and *by* are free morphemes. In contrast, morphemes such as past *-ed* and continuous *–ing* are not independent words and, thus, not free morphemes. See **bound morpheme**.

**functional morpheme** – A subclass of morpheme whose linguistic purpose is more grammatical and language-internal than to refer to things in the world. Verbal *-s* as in *Harry loves pizza* is functional; its purpose is a grammatical quirk of English whereby verbs must agree with their third-person singular subject with the agreement suffix *-s*. See **lexical morpheme**.

**fusional** – A fusional language, also called an inflectional language, is one with affixes that carry multiple meanings and/or functions. The *-s* suffix on English verbs is a single morpheme comprising the features for third-person singular subject, present tense, indicative mood.

**gerund** – In English, the *-ing* form of a verb that functions as a noun, as in *I like swimming*. Not to be confused with the identically pronounced present participle form, as in *We are swimming*, which is a verb.

**grammar** – The system underlying a speaker's knowledge of a language, including the morphemes of the language, the morphological rules for combining them, the sound system of the language, the rules for making sentences and the semantic system generally of matching linguistic expressions to meaning. See **descriptive grammar** and **descriptive grammar**.

**grammatical** – An expression is grammatical if it follows the unconscious rules speakers have about their language. *Buddy likes to eat mice* is a grammatical sentence while *\*To likes mice Buddy eat* is not.

**grammatical word** – A form of a word in a lexeme that fulfills a particular grammatical function. The two forms *cat* and *cats* are two grammatical words, singular *cat* and plural *cats*, of the lexeme √CAT.

**head** – In compounds, the morpheme that specifies the category of the compound and that semantically identifies the class that's restricted by a modifier. The compound noun *keychain* comprises the head *chain* and the modifier *key*; *chain*, a noun, tells us that the compound *keychain* is a noun, and *key* narrows down what kind of chain is being referred to.

**historical linguistics** – The branch of linguistics that investigates language change through time. By working backwards, historical linguists work out earlier forms a language. Historical linguistics is intimately connected to comparative linguistics.

**homonym, homophone, homophony** – Two morphemes that sound the same but have clearly different meanings are homonyms. *Bat*, the flying mammal, is homophonous with *bat*, the stick used in baseball and cricket.

**imperative** – A form of verb used for ordering, commanding and suggesting. There's no special imperative form in English. In the sentences *Go!* and *Mow the lawn!*, the verbs *go* and *mow* are imperative.

**inclusive** – A first-person plural form, particularly in pronouns, that includes the speaker and the hearer. English lacks morphology for this distinction, but the inclusive meaning is 'we, i.e., me and you', while the exclusive meaning is 'we, me and someone other than you'. See **exclusive**.

**Indo-European** – The family of related languages to which English belongs. Indo-European includes most of the languages of Europe, Iran and surrounding areas, and northern India, and the earlier forms of those languages, including the mother of them all: Proto-Indo-European. Through colonialism and related kinds of expansionism, Indo-European languages such as Spanish, English, Portuguese, French and Russian have spread to the Americas and parts of Africa and Asia.

**infinitive** – A nonfinite verbal form typically used in certain subordinate clauses. English infinitives are usually accompanied with *to*, as in *to go*, *to eat* and *to accuse*.

**infix** – An affix that appears within a root. In Chamorro, *tristi* means 'sad'. While English makes a noun by suffixing *-ness* to the root, Chamorro inserts *in* inside the root: *tr-in-isti* 'sadness'. As a result of the infixation, the root becomes discontinuous.

**inflection** – A process of wordformation that produces the different grammatical forms of words called for by the syntax of the sentence. Noun inflections include number (singular and plural) and, in many languages, case marking. Verbs inflect for tense and agreement, among other things.

**inflectional morpheme** – A morpheme that relates a wordform to other wordforms in the same lexeme. Plural *-s* is an inflectional morpheme added to nouns.

**inflectional morphology** – The part of the morphological system that accounts for wordforms within a lexeme. Inflectional morphology generates various forms of the lexeme $\sqrt{\text{WALK}}$: *walk, walks, walked and walking*, each associated with one or more grammatical meanings and functions.

**lexeme** – The collection of wordforms related by inflectional morphology. The lexeme for the verb *go* includes *go, goes, went, going* and *gone*.

**isolating** – A language is isolating when it has very little morphology. In an isolating language each word tends to be a single morpheme.

**lexical morpheme** – One broad subclass of morphemes, those with semantic content often involving reference to things and events in the world, including internal thoughts and feelings. The clearest examples of lexical morphemes are nouns, verbs, adjectives, adverbs and at least some prepositions. Lexical morphemes contrast with **functional morphemes**.

**lexicalized** – An expression becomes lexicalized when it becomes a word or phrase that is stored as a unit.

**lexicon** – The list of minimal sound-meaning pairs in a language, including single morphemes and multimorphemic forms that have meanings not predictable from their components. Certainly *bird* is a morpheme in the lexicon, but the compound bimorphemic *blackbird* can also be considered to be in the lexicon. In sign language, a morpheme is the collection of pairs of meanings and visual signs.

**morpheme** – A morpheme is the smallest unit of meaning and function in a language, a minimal sound-meaning pair. The word *tree* is a single morpheme, while *trees* is two morphemes, *tree* and the plural marker -*s*. The complex word *institutionalize* arguably contains at least four morphemes: *institute*, -*(t)ion*, -*al* and -*ize*. In sign languages, a morpheme is a minimal pairing between meaning and visual sign.

**morphology** – Morphology is the part of the grammar responsible for wordformation. The word also refers to the scientific study of that component of the grammar. English morphology suffixes -*s* to most nouns to make plurals: *cat-s*. Ilocano morphology can make plural nouns by repeating part of the word: *bato* ('stone' )⇒ *bat-bato* ('stones').

**morphophonolgy** – The interaction of morphology and phonology. We might consider an abstract representation of the regular English plural morpheme as /z/. This morpheme interacts with phonology and is pronounced as [z], [s] or [əz], depending on the last sound of the word it attaches to.

**morphosyntax** – Morphology and syntax when considered as a combined system. In the sentence *Esmerelda likes ice cream*, the word *likes* is formed by morphologically combining *like* with the third-person singular suffix -*s*, but that morphology is syntactically dependent on the third-person singular subject *Esmerelda*.

**nominative** – A case marking usually indicating the subject of a tensed sentence. *She* is the feminine nominative pronoun, as in *She plays the alto sax*.

**nonconcatenative morphology** – Morphology involving morphemes that don't string out in a linear fashion. In Lomca, *gè* the first-person pronoun corresponding to the English word *I* used for present tense has both linear and nonconcatenative morphology. The sequence *g-e* is linear, but the high tone is added on top of the vowel segment. Arabic and other Semitic languages include nonconcatenative morphology, mixing roots of a string of consonants interspersed with vowels indicating different forms of the root.

**noun** – A word category for denoting individual things, multiple things or stuff, commonly defined as the name for a person, place or thing. In *Dani ate the pizza*, *Dani* and *pizza* are nouns.

**noun incorporation** – A particular kind of morphosyntactic incorporation in which what's otherwise an independent noun or other words becomes part of a verb. In *Pat plowed snow*, the direct object *snow* is an independent word. Something like incorporation appears in the verb *snow-plow*, in which *snow* is part of the verb.

**number** – A category of morpheme used for indicating whether the noun is singular or plural, etc. The noun *cat* has no marking for singular; *cats* uses the regular English plural suffix. Some languages have morphology to make more nonsingular distinctions such as dual, trial and paucal.

**paradigm** – The collection of different grammatical forms of a words, typically presented in a list or table. The present tense paradigm of English *sing* is *I sing; you sing; she, he* and *it sings; we sing, you* (plural) *sing; they sing.*

**participle** – A verb form used with auxiliary or so-called helping verbs. The perfect participle may be a regular *-ed* form or an irregular form, as in *I have decided* and *I had written*, where *decided* and *written* are the perfect participles. English passive participles, as in *the book was written by a committee*, are identical in form to perfect participles. Another participle is the present or progressive participle, which has an *-ing* form, as in *Sheila is writing a novel.*

**passive** – A verbal form using, in English, the passive participle and the auxiliary *be*, as in t*he senator was convicted of taking bribes*, with the *was* form of *be* and the participle *convicted*. The subject of the sentence corresponds to the thing being acted on by the verb. Some languages add an affix to make the verb passive. See **active**.

**paucal** – Number morphology to indicate a few of something. In Lihir, *gol* means 'you two', *gotol* means 'you three', while *gehet* means 'a few but more than three'.

**perfect participle** – The participle used with the auxiliary *have* to show past activity that is still relevant for the present, as in *we have arrived*.

**person** – For the most part we can talk of three persons that can be referred to in language. When speakers refer to themselves, the reference is first person; the English words *I*, *me* and *myself* are first-person pronouns. When speakers refer to or address the individual they're talking with (the addressee), that reference is second person; *you* is the second-person pronoun. When speakers refer to anyone or anything outside themselves and the addressee, that reference is third person; *she*, *he*, *it*, *her*, *him*, *they* and *them* are all third-person pronouns. Ordinary nouns are also third person; both *the cat* and *the mouse* are third-person references in the sentence *the cat ate the mouse*.

**phonestheme** – A sound or sequence of sounds that suggest a meaning but not quite precisely enough to be a morpheme. The *gl-* sequence in *glitter*, *gleam*, *glisten*, etc. is a phonestheme.

**phonetics** – The physical properties of language sounds and how they're produced and perceived. It's also the study of those properties. The sound [d] is phonetically described as the front part of the tongue coming in contact with the alveolar ridge to, briefly, cut off the outward airflow from the oral tract while the vocal cords are vibrating.

**phonology** – The rules and patterns of how sounds interact and the study of those rules and patterns. In English, /p/, pronounced with the two lips coming together, is accompanied by a puff of air when the lips release the sound, as in the word *pit*. But that same English /p/ doesn't have a puff of air when it's preceded by /s/, as in *spit*.

**phrase** – A group of one or more words behaving like a unit. *Smelly dogs* is a noun phrase, a noun modified by an adjective. *The smelly dogs* is a larger phrase. *The smelly dogs next door* is yet a longer phrase. Phrases can also be single words, such as *they* or *them*.

All of these phrases behave like the same unit in the grammar; for example, they can all be the subject or object of a sentence: *Julie doesn't like {smelly dogs/the smelly dogs/the smelly dogs next door/them}*.

**plural** – Number morphology to indicate more than one of something, as *-s* in *cats*. Some languages make finer plural distinctions. See **dual**, **trial**, **paucal**.

**portmanteau morpheme** – A morpheme that stands for two or more meanings. Plural *-s* in English contributes one meaning to the verb, [Past]. In contrast, the *-s* agreement morpheme is a portmanteau. In the sentence *Farzad loves pizza*, the *-s* in *loves* is at least [Present Tense, 3rd person singular subject, Indicative mood].

**postposition** – A word category like prepositions but occurring after a phrase. Japanese has postpositions, as in *ie de* ('house in'). Postpositions are a kind of adposition.

**prefix** – An affix that precedes the stem. *Unscientific* contains the prefix *un-* attached to the stem *scientific*.

**preposition** – A word category typically indicating spatial, temporal or directional relationships. Prepositions include words such as *in*, *on*, *with*, *to* and *for*. Prepositions come before phrases, as in *for the children*, *to Ryan*. Prepositions are a kind of adposition.

**prescriptive grammar** – Rules and advice usually about writing but also about speaking so-called 'proper' language. Teachers, editors and sticklers for schoolroom grammar prescribe how, they think, we should speak and write. Prescriptivists might say *ain't* isn't a word and caution against what we should end a sentence with. Many prescriptive rules are helpful for writing clearly and efficiently, but they sometimes don't accord with descriptive grammar.

**priming experiments** – In psycholinguistics, an experimental technique of providing a stimulus to experiment participants and measuring responses. If primed or prompted with the word *black*, people are statistically much more likely to respond with the word *white* than with *purple* or *mountain*, for example.

**productive morpheme/productivity** – A morpheme is productive if it's used by speakers to create new words. Plural *-s* is productive;

if a new noun enters the language, speakers automatically know they can pluralize it with -*s*. On the other hand, -*th* is not productive; while there are a number of words containing -*th*, such as *wealth*, *truth* and *depth*, speakers of modern English no longer use -*th* in creative wordformation.

**Proto-Indo-European** – The ancestor language of all the Indo-European languages.

**psycholinguistics** – The study of the interaction between language and cognitive processing. Psycholinguists want to know how words are stored and accessed and how larger units of language such as sentences are processed for meaning.

**root** – An unanalyzable, monomorphemic form, free or bound, that's left when all affixes are removed. Words may have more than one root. If -*ation* is removed from *wordformation*, the remaining roots are √WORD and √FORM. As described in this book, the root is abstract; for morphology to occur, we assume the root converts into a stem.

**semantics** – That part of the grammar that attributes meaning to words and sentences. For example, in the sentence *Emma wants to go to the opera*, according to the syntax, the semantics is that it's Emma that is the subject of *to go*, even though the word *Emma* doesn't appear near that verb.

**simple word** – A word comprising one morpheme, such as *simple*, *word*, *bug*, *lift*, *bird* and *green*, as opposed to complex words, which have more than one morpheme: *reword*, *buggy*, *birdlike* and *greenish*.

**singular** – Number morphology to indicate one of something. While English generally uses -*s* for plural, it has no marking for the singular: *cat/cats*.

**stem** – Any wordbuilding unit to which wordformation applies. A root becomes a basic stem as it undergoes wordformation. Stems can be iterative. The root √HAPPY forms a stem *happy* to which the prefix *un*- may be added to form *unhappy*. In turn, *unhappy* can be the stem to which is added -*ness* to form *unhappiness*.

**stress** – A psychological and phonological phenomenon of loudness on a syllable relative to the loudness of other nearby syllables. The loudness is usually accompanied by higher pitch in the voice as well. The word *carrot* has stress on the first syllable while *baboon* is stressed on the final syllable.

**suffix** – An affix that follows the stem. The regular English past tense *-ed* is a suffix, as in *paint-ed*. In Crow, *-k* indicates that the verb it's attached to is understood as a declarative statement.

**superlative** – A form of an adjective, such as *the most* or *the highest degree*. Short adjectives form the superlative with the suffix *-est*, as in *greenest*; longer adjectives use the word *most* before the adjective, as in *most interesting*.

**suppletion** – The relationship between forms in a lexeme that have no obvious morphological relationship. The present/past contrast in *go/went* is suppletive, as is the *people* plural of *person*.

**switch reference marker** – A morpheme that informs whether the subjects in two clauses are the same or different. The Siouan language Crow suffixes *-ák* at the end of a verb to indicate that the following verb has the same subject. The suffix *-m* informs that the subject of the next verb is different.

**syntax** – The rules for assembling morphemes and words into sentences. The syntax of English generally calls for the subject to come first in a simple declarative sentence, followed by the verb and any objects: *the cat ate the mouse*. Persian syntax puts the object between the subject and verb: *gorbeh muš-o xord*, literally 'cat mouse-the ate'.

**synthetic compound** – A compound headed by a noun derived from a verb, such as *hunter*, and a modifier that acts like a direct object like *duck* in *duck hunter*. A synthetic compound can be described as including a head that's derived from a verb and a modifier that is an argument of the verb; usually, the argument is a direct object. Typically, the *-er* suffix, usually indicating someone who does the verb, is added to the verb to derive a noun that heads the compound, for example *hunter*, *writer* and *watcher*, derived from *hunt*, *write* and *watch*.

**tense** – A category or morpheme used usually with verbs to indicate time. Common tenses are present, past and future. Tense is often expressed as an adposition to the verb. In English, past tense for regular verbs is *-ed*.

**tone** – Tones are vocal pitches that can change lexical meaning while the consonants and vowels remain the same. In Thai, *ná:* with a high tone means 'young maternal uncle or aunt', while *nà:* with a low tone means 'nickname'. (The : indicates that the preceding vowel is long.) Thai has a total of five tones (Fromkin et al. 2014, 212).

**toneme** – A tone that, by itself, is a morpheme. In Mono-Bili, a language of Congo, high tone by itself, used on top of sounds, is the past tense marker, while a low tone marks future tense. For example, *dá* means 'spanked', while *dà* means 'will spank'.

**trial** – Number morphology to indicate three of something, in contrast to other kinds of plural. In Lihir, *gol* means 'you two' and *gotol* means 'you three'.

**typology** – The study of similarities and differences across languages. Typology is important for informing us about what languages, in general, prefer to do and not do. For example, one study of 702 languages found that 496 languages had a predominant or moderate preference for using suffixes over prefixes, 146 languages favored prefixes and the other 130 languages used prefixes and suffixes roughly equally. The typological generalization that more than 70% of languages in the sample with the rest roughly split between a prefixing preference or no preference suggests that the English preference for putting *-ed* at the end of the verb is probably not a random idiosyncrasy of English.

**ungrammatical** – An expression that doesn't follow the unconscious rules speakers have about their language is ungrammatical. *\*Mice eat to Buddy likes* is ungrammatical, not English.

**verb** – A word category for denoting events or states. In *Dani ate the pizza*, the verb is *ate*.

**word family** – A word family is a group of lexemes with a root in common. *Write, rewrite* and *writer* constitute a family of words with the root √WRITE in common.

**wordform** – A morphophonological variant within a lexeme. The lexeme *give* contains the wordforms *give, gives, gave, giving* and *given*. The preposition *on* has a single wordform.

**zero derivation** – The supposed conversion of one grammatical form of a morpheme to another without any overt morphology. If *walk* is a verb, the identical noun form *walk* can be zero-derived from the verb.

# Chapter 1

# Introduction

## 1.1 Preliminaries

What's the longest word in English? Schoolchildren and plenty of other people might drag out that old warhorse *antidisestablishmentarianism*, weighing in at 28 letters. That figure of 28 letters is a measure of the written language. Linguists, more interested in spoken language, will point out that the two letters *sh* in the middle of the word count as one sound. So, the length of the word dwindles from 28 letters to 27 sounds. Still, that's pretty long – way longer than words we typically use in daily conversation. Even for a technical word, it's long; in fact, it's longer than a lot of sentences, including the sentence: *that's a long word*.

But is it the longest word? Do some internet searching, and in 0.67 seconds, you'll be able to access a short list of long words headed by *pneumonoultramicroscopicsilicovolcanoconiosis*, with 43 sounds and 45 letters. The word supposedly refers to a silica-dust lung disease, but it's probably used more often as an example of a really big word than it is to refer to the disease. On this list *antidisestablishmentarianism* pulls in at sixth place. Do a little more searching, and you'll find that *pneumonoultramicroscopicsilicovolcanoconiosis* itself is quickly dethroned by some absurdly long words, such as the chemical name of a gargantuan protein that would reportedly take three hours to pronounce. Thankfully, there are shorter ways of referring to this protein, including the word *titin*, which takes a breezy 0.382 seconds to articulate as an isolated word out of context.

DOI: 10.4324/9781003030188-1

But back to the demoted *antidisestablishmentarianism*. Although it's not the longest word in English, we can easily make longer words out of it. According to the second edition of *The Random House Dictionary of the English Language* published in 1987 (aging, I know, but still useful), it means "opposition to the withdrawal of state support or recognition from an established church, esp. the Anglican Church in 19th-century England". If that's the case, then support of such opposition could be described as *proantidisestablishmentarianism*, a word formed simply by appending *pro-* to the beginning. Further, if such opposition to withdrawing state support from an established church were qualified by certain political, legal or other technicalities, that opposition could be termed *quasiantidisestablishmentarianism*, in which *quasi-* sort of means, well, 'sort of'. And if the opposition were disingenuous, it could be called *pseudoantidisestablishmentarianism*, while the opposing ideology could be referred to as *antiantidisestablishmentarianism*. As the two *anti*s seem to cancel each other out, *antiantidisestablishmentarianism* must, therefore, mean the same as *disestablishmentarianism* but perhaps with a little added emphasis on 'againstness'.

Are these four extensions of *antidisestablishmentarianism* really words? They might not be listed in dictionaries but being listed in a dictionary isn't a necessary criterion for wordhood, and in any case, you *can* find them in use, at least as musings about long words if not as particularly helpful contributions to political discourse.

The four extensions of our original *antidisestablishmentarianism* are attested, that is, with a record of someone somewhere having used them. However, I hadn't known of their existence before starting to write this opening chapter. Independently and creatively, I invented them, though it's probably more precise to say that they existed as potential words and that I discovered them. And though not particularly useful words, they're not nonsense either. As words with easily recognized pieces, it's not difficult to see how they're put together from those pieces, and, as for meaning, if you know what *antidisestablishmentarianism* means and if you know how to use *pro-*, *quasi-* and *pseudo-* and that you can repeat the *anti-*, then you, as a fellow speaker of the language, can arrive at a pretty good approximation of the meaning of the extended words. And even if your understanding of the word *antidisestablishmentarianism* is hazy at best, you do know that *antiantidisestablishmentarianism* is its opposite.

We know what the pieces mean and how to use them because they're part of our vocabulary, and they appear in other contexts that provide a pattern that feeds as well as reflects our understanding. Take *pro-*. It's a common enough piece that appears in *prolife*, *prochoice*, *proimmigration*, *pronationalism*, *prounionist* and about 500 other words that Random House listed some decades ago, and we can surmise that more have been attested since then. Random House also listed some 600 *quasi-* words, including *quasi-temporal*, *quasi-wrong*, *quasi-zealous*, and more than 300 *pseudo-* words such as *pseudoacademic*, *pseudocourteous* and *pseudozoological*. By the way, Random House didn't bother defining these 1,400-some words, which are in the dictionary, apparently, just for the record; the dictionary writers reasonably assuming that if you know what *X, Y* and *Z* mean, then you can figure out what *pro-X, quasi-Y* and *pseudo-Z* mean. Meanings that are deducible like this are **compositional** in that if you know the meanings of the parts and you know the grammatical rules of a language for putting them together, then you can predict the meaning of the whole. Not all words of more than one piece are fully compositional, and many words of more than one piece are not compositional at all, but there's a general assumption that compositionality plays some role in the architecture of wordformation. Words comprising a single piece are **simple words**; words with more than one piece are **complex**.

We could continue finding ways to extend *antidisestablishmentarianism* into longer words, but let's work in the other direction. Not only can we compose words by joining pieces together, but we can decompose words into smaller bits. In *antidisestablishmentarianism*, we've already identified *anti-* as a piece, and it's easy to pick out the other pieces, as in (1), along with other words in which the pieces appear. Note that we're using the hyphens as part of a linguistics convention to indicate boundaries between pieces in complex words. A hyphen on the right means that the piece attaches to something on its right, and vice versa for hyphens on the left.

(1) dis-        disagree, disrupt, displace, dishonest, disrespect
    establish   established, establishes, establishing, reestablish
    -ment       government, bewilderment, pavement, environment, inducement
    -arian      parliamentarian, disciplinarian, contrarian
    -ism        capitalism, atheism, industrialism, wokism, marxism

The precise meaning of the pieces isn't always clear. In *dishonest* and *disagree*, *dis-* has a negative sort of meaning that's absent in *disrupt* and *displace*. That could suggest that there's more than one *dis-* in English with different meanings but just happen to sound the same, like *blue* and *blew*. The variant or vague meanings of some morphemes will be discussed in the next chapter.

Given our observations about both building up and taking apart words, we come to the conclusion that words are composed of smaller units. Not all words, of course, as many of them are simple and unanalyzable, such as *cat, red, sleep* and *with* and many others. While a word like *establishment* is analyzable into at least two pieces, each with a meaning and/or function that, compositionally, contributes to the whole, *sleep* cannot be analyzed, for example, into *sl* and *eep*, as neither *sl* nor *eep* has a meaning or function of its own.

Thus, as speakers of English, we generally know the units that make up words. Our linguistic knowledge includes at least how to pronounce those units and, at least roughly, what they mean. Let's return to *pro-*. We know how to pronounce it (rhymes with *throw*) and that it means something like 'in favor of, supporting, for'. In addition, importantly, we know something about its word-building properties; that is, we know how to combine it with other pieces. For example, each of the four pieces we used to extend *antidisestablishmentarianism* precedes rather than follows the word. Observe the contrast between the grammatical, and attested, words in (2a) and the ungrammatical examples in (2b) where we tried adding the bits to the end of the word. Not only are they unattested, but they're ungrammatical, which is why they're unattested. The asterisk (*) is a convention in linguistics to indicate an ungrammatical expression, something that's not part of the language and, in fact, can't be because it's ruled out by the grammar.

(2a)  **pro**antidisestablishmentarianism
      **quasi**antidisestablishmentarianism
      **pseudo**antidisestablishmentarianism
      **anti**antidisestablishmentarianism
(2b)  *antidisestablishmentarianism**pro**
      *antidisestablishmentarianism**quasi**
      *antidisestablishmentarianism**pseudo**
      *antidisestablishmentarianism**anti**

Assuming that the grammaticality contrasts between the sample data in (2a) and (2b) are not just a few oddballs but, rather, are representative of a much larger set of data, we propose a descriptive generalization about English that *pro-*, *quasi-*, *pseudo-* and *anti-* must go at the beginning but not at the end of the chunk that we want to build on. Hence, the hyphen is at the right edge of the pieces listed in (1), aside from *establish*, which is the core to be built on. That is, besides knowing pronunciation and meaning, we also know something about the grammar of how to combine these pieces with others. Part of our overall knowledge about the interaction of sound, meaning and grammar in the language we speak concerns wordformation, which is what this book is about.

## 1.2 Words and Grammar and What We Know about Them

The part of the grammar that deals with wordformation is called **morphology**. Or, more succinctly, morphology is the grammar of words (e.g., Booij 2009, 1; Audring and Masini 2019, 2). In terms of goals of what a theory of morphology should do, Aronoff (1976) identified the task of morphologists as "the enumeration of the class of possible words of a language", which, in plainer English, means identifying all the words in a language that can be built with the available components of words. As such, morphology is one of the components of the grammar of any language.

A **grammar** of a language is a system that allows speakers to produce and understand the words and sentences of their language. This system of knowledge is largely unconscious. Speakers use their language knowledge quite efficiently and effectively, but, despite the boring lessons suffered through in school about gerunds, superlatives and dangling prepositions, as speakers, we really don't understand in any explicit way what we're doing when we speak and listen to language. This state of affairs is analogous to other skills and knowledge we possess. Most anyone can learn how to ride a bicycle, but our skill at bike riding is far exceeded by our utter ineptitude at explicitly stating what's involved in doing it. Except for specialists, none of us is in any position to accurately explain the physical mechanics, the muscular coordination, the neurological infrastructure of the inner ear and the cerebellum, the visual feedback from the world rushing by and how all those things work together in allowing us to balance and propel forward on a bicycle. Similarly, whatever language skills speakers have, they typically don't have the wherewithal to describe the grammar that underlies those skills. However, the analogy between language and bike riding breaks down on an important point: bike riders don't *really* know what they're doing, but there are physiologists and other experts who do have a pretty good idea about how balancing on a bicycle works. Similarly, speakers can't articulate how language works, but, in contrast to the expertise of physiologists, linguists, the people whose goal it is to understand the workings of language, sit in a much shakier position than the physiologists. There are grammatical descriptions of many languages and general theories about purported principles that may underlie all languages, but linguists are far from reaching any consensus on an overarching theory to account for the grammar of any particular language, let alone a broad theory of language. Nonetheless, even if the science of linguistics is still very much a work in progress, linguists have offered good descriptions of linguistic phenomena and observations of the similarities and differences across languages.

To start somewhere, any spoken language is made up of a set of sounds – a subset of all the possible sounds that are used in the languages of the world. Individual sounds are typically not meaningful, but sequences of sounds are. The sounds represented by *c, a, t* in the conventional English spelling of the word *cat* don't mean anything individually, but the three-sound sequence in the order *c-a-t*, represented as [kæt] in the International Phonetic Alphabet, does. It refers to felines, most commonly to domestic felines but also, depending on context, to the larger class of animals that encompasses lions, tigers, leopards, lynxes and cheetahs as well. Not all languages use sounds. In the case of sign languages, such as American Sign Language, signers use a visual medium, including, among other things, hand and arm shape, position and movement instead of sound. But the focus in this book is morphology in sound-based language.

The sound system comprises **phonetics**, the physical properties of sounds and how they're articulated and perceived, and **phonology**, the system of how sounds interact to produce what we actually say and hear in spoken language. For example, the words in (3a) are pronounceable according to the available sounds in English and the language's phonological rules, and, in fact, they happen to be English words. The sound sequences in (3b) are also phonologically legitimate and, although not words, they *could* be words. For example, in the context of Star Trek, a worg could be a baby Borg. However, the sound sequences in (3c) are not possible English words because they violate English phonology, specifically constraints on which sounds can go together where; for example, English words don't start with the sound sequences *wd*, *ns* or *mg*.

(3a)  word, sentence, grammar
(3b)  worg, zentence, rammarg
(3c)  *wdro, *nsetence, *mgraamr

The part of the grammar that builds sentences out of words is the **syntax** of the language. The syntax produces (4a) as a legitimate sentence but disallows (4b), which is not an English sentence.

(4a)  Antidisestablishmentarianism is an English word.
(4b)  *Word an is English antidisestablishmentarianism.

Once the words, each with its own word semantics, are in a legitimate syntactic structure, the **semantics**, or meaning, of the sentence can be determined. For example, besides the individual meanings of the words *Emma*, *saw* and *her*, the syntax of English tells us that *her* in (5) can refer to any female thing in the universe except Emma.

(5)  Emma saw her.

Based on the introductory descriptions of the components of grammar so far, we might propose a very simple first approximation of how the components collaborate in a model of the grammar, something like the following schema.

(6)  sounds  ⇒  word pieces  ⇒  words  ⇒  sentences
                                    ⇑              ⇑
                              *morphology*      *syntax*

However, this simple linear model is woefully inaccurate, to say the least. First, the semantics aren't indicated. That's partly because meaning is determined in several places, at least at the level of words and then at the level of larger phrases and sentences. Meaning, therefore, interacts with the grammar in more than one place.

A second problem is that it isn't the case that the morphology builds words that simply feed into the syntax, as suggested in (6). Rather, the morphology and syntax are tightly connected in what's called the **morphosyntax**. As an example of how morphology and syntax work together, compare the grammatical sentence in (7a) with the ungrammatical version in (7b), in which *rains* is plural and, therefore, inconsistent with the singular verb form *stays*.

(7a)   The rain in Spain **stays** mainly in the plain.
(7b)   *The rains in Spain **stays** mainly in the plain.

The verb *stays* is made of two pieces *stay* and -*s*. The morphology, the wordformation component of the grammar, takes care of putting the two pieces together, making sure the -*s* follows rather than precedes the verb. But adding -*s* to the verb follows from the verb's syntactic relation to the singular subject that precedes it – *the rain in Spain*.

(8)   [The rain in Spain] **stays** mainly in the plain
           ⇑                              ⇑
        3.Sg      ⇒      3.Sg verb
       subject            (in present tense)

If the subject is plural, the form *stay*, without the -*s*, is required.

(9)   [The rains in Spain] **stay** mainly in the plain
           ⇑                            ⇑
      non-3.Sg    ⇒    non-3.Sg verb
      subject              (in present tense)

Again, the morphology of the verb depends on the verb's syntactic relation to the subject of the sentence.

Another objection to the oversimplicity of the model suggested in (6) stems from the interaction between morphology and sound. A transparent example is the English plural. There are a good many irregular plural forms in English – irregular in that they aren't predictable and simply have to be memorized. Here are a few.

(10)    child/children, goose/geese, mouse/mice, sheep/sheep

However, most nouns have predictable forms for their plural, corresponding to the addition of -s or -es in conventional spelling. The plurals spelled with -s have two distinct pronunciations. For the words in (11a), the -s is pronounced, well, like an s, [s], while the plurals in (11b) are pronounced with a [z] sound. The third pronunciation of the regular plural, as in the examples in (11c), corresponds to the plurals written with -es and are pronounced [əz], like the [z] sound with an intervening schwa-like sound. We'll explain [z], [s], [əz] and other symbols in Section 1.4; for now, just recognize that the plurals are pronounced differently in each set of examples in (11).

(11a)   [s]-plurals:    lips, maps, cats, parts, peaks, books
(11b)   [z]-plurals:    cabs, ribs, lids, creeds, dogs, cogs
(11c)   [əz]-plurals:   churches, latches, judges, midges, horses, mazes, rashes, leashes

The choice of which plural goes on which nouns is very regular and predictable: [s] after the sounds of the p, t and k that precede the plural marker in the words in (11a); [z] after the b, d and g that end the singular forms in (11b); and the [əz], that sounds something like *uhz*, for the sounds that end *church, judge*, etc. in (11c). The presence of these three variant pronunciations of the plural is not random; rather, the choice of plural depends on the sound it's attached to, very systematically. This interaction of the morphology with the sound system is **morphophonology**.

The schema in (6) is, therefore, incomplete and incorrect in a number of ways. Grammar isn't a linear sequence of discrete components, one feeding into the next; the phonology, morphology, syntax and semantics are not independent modules but, rather, interact in many ways. Nonetheless, in this book, the focus is on the morphology, the wordformation component. To some degree, descriptively, we're pretending that we can focus on morphology independent of the other components. Where relevant, however, interaction of morphology with other parts of the grammar is discussed.

An expression in accord with the morphological, syntactic and phonological requirements of a language is **grammatical**. Anything that doesn't follow from the grammar is **ungrammatical**. As mentioned above, linguists are still far from adequately articulating what the grammatical rules are. Nonetheless, as speakers, we do generally have a good intuitive feel for what's grammatical and what isn't. If we didn't, we wouldn't be able to use the language. Repeating the following examples, you don't need to be a linguist, grammarian, English grammar teacher, or a publishing house stylist to know which of the following two sentences is ungrammatical.

(12a)   Antidisestablishmentarianism is an English word.
(12b)   *Word an is English antidisestablishmentarianism.

## 1.3  Knowledge of Language

We've been referring to speakers' knowledge, what they know, unconsciously, about their language. An average speaker knows what *establish* means and how it's pronounced, knows that it's a verb and knows how it can compose with *-ment* to form the noun *establishment* and, conversely, that *establishment* can be decomposed into two pieces, each with a meaning and function. In Section 1.2, knowledge of language was compared with the knowledge of how to ride a bicycle – the similarity being that they're both skills that, perhaps, specialists can accurately describe but whose details are unknown to most people who speak languages and ride bicycles.

In modern linguistic theory, particularly in the assumptions underlying the generative tradition of Noam Chomsky since the 1950s, a speaker's knowledge consists of a lexicon of, roughly speaking, words AND a computational system for combining the words into sentences and gleaning meaning from them such that streams of language sound are associated with specific meanings. The term generative refers to a proposed algorithmic system of language rules that takes the words and *generates* all and only the sentences of a language. This knowledge of the generative relationship between sound and meaning is internalized in a speaker's brain. Another way to see language is to think of one as a set of utterances, an infinitely large set, which can be observed and analyzed to try to understand what a speaker's knowledge is. That is, by studying utterances – sentences – that speakers produce (along with nonutterances – things that speakers don't say), linguists try to discover what speakers' computational system is by reverse-engineering the utterances. Much of the grammar is language-specific, most obviously the lexicon of words, but also the ways to make words, the ways to make sentences and the choice of sounds and how they're put together. For example, the future tense of English verbs differs from the future in Crow. But generativists also hold to the view that some of a speaker's knowledge is common to all languages as a genetically coded, prewired biological endowment, independent of, yet related to, other aspects of cognition. On this view, certain aspects of language parallel the genetic coding of, say, the visual or hearing system. Other linguists disagree, seeing knowledge of language as an extension of cognitive abilities generally, without any language-specific properties.

However, both generativists and nongenerativists recognize, despite the many, apparently, huge differences among languages, that crosslinguistic patterns do emerge and that these patterns must be reflecting important things about the human capacity for language. In morphology as well as in other areas of linguistics, languages tend to do some things and not do other things. Whatever the reasons for languages' preferences for certain patterns, they must play into our knowledge of language. Discussion of knowledge of language runs throughout the generativist-based literature. Chomsky titled one of his books – surprise, surprise! – *Knowledge of Language*, but he specifically addresses what he means by knowledge of language in much of his work. A succinct discussion can be found in Freidin (2012, 16–22).

Given that this knowledge of language is overwhelmingly unconscious knowledge, it's the job of linguists to articulate exactly what that knowledge is. The prime concern of linguists is the spoken language. While data in the form of written language do sometimes comes into play, written language is a different skill that children laboriously learn after they've pretty well mastered spoken language. And in contrast to learning how to read and write, children master their first language (and sometimes more than one language) without specific instruction and, it is often said, do so effortlessly. Further, written language and literacy bring to bear an important distinction between **prescriptive grammar** and **descriptive grammar**. Grammar in the prescriptive sense is what most of us think of: the dreadfully boring instructions and seemingly pointless advice that we get from English classes, picky teachers, editors and style manuals – don't split infinitives, don't start a sentence with *and*, don't end a sentence with a preposition – all of which speakers violate with abandon in ordinary conversation. Yet prescriptive admonitions live on. It's surprising, in an age of informality, that Introduction to Linguistics students question the grammaticality of a sentence like that in (13a).

(13a)   Who'd you give the money to?
(13b)   To whom did you give the money?

The objection stems from an apparently still taught prescriptive rule admonishing against ending a sentence with a preposition. But if you pay attention to what people say instead of what you think they *should* say, speakers, even those who claim they don't end sentences with prepositions, are overwhelmingly more likely to ask, '*Who'd you give the money to?*' than its prescriptive alternative, which also, by the way, contains the prescriptive and moribund *whom*.

Linguists take a descriptive approach, being much more interested in observing and trying to understand what speakers actually do than in telling speakers what they should or shouldn't do. A linguist would no more tell a speaker not to end a sentence with a preposition than a biologist would tell a bird not to fly. On verbal morphology, a prescriptivist may advise that the past tense of the verb *dive* is *dived*; a descriptivist, in contrast, observes that speakers say both *dived* and *dove* (rhymes with *stove*).

This isn't to say that prescriptive and descriptive grammars are fundamentally opposed. For the most part, they align. For example, both prescriptive and descriptive grammars tell us that English adjectives generally precede the nouns they modify: *big fish* rather than *\*fish big*. But when a prescriptivist points out a supposed mistake, a descriptivist leans on the side of speakers' grammatical capacity. Let's look at a specific example to get a feel for the difference in attitude and approach between someone proselytizing how people should use language and someone trying to understand how language works by describing how people talk. Both prescriptivists and descriptivists will note a certain oddity about *'That's the guy who his mother was my intro to lit professor'*. If you included that sentence in a school paper, your English teacher would no doubt hand back the following editorial, i.e., prescriptive correction.

(14)  That's the woman ~~who her~~ whose mother was my intro to lit professor,

A linguist, however, is more likely to react with, 'Hmmm, that's interesting'. English, of course, does have the pronoun *whose* that functions just as the English teacher recommends, but in ordinary speech, people do occasionally produce *who her, who his* and *who their* instead of *whose*, in a very systematic way not simply as a careless error that reflects the deterioration of the language and communication leading to the impending doom of civilization. From the point of view of linguists, there's grammar underlying the *who her* construction. That 'mistake', interestingly, is probably related to a fact known to linguists who focus on crosslinguistic patterns in the field of **typology**. A relative pronoun like *whose* is much less common across languages than ordinary pronouns like *who*; languages seemingly prefer to separate the *who* meaning from a possessive piece like *his*. The fact that people sometimes say *who her* instead of *whose* is much more than supposed sloppiness or ignorance; it reveals something very deep about language – a crosslinguistic generalization about languages surfacing in a particular construction in English.

People may opine that *ain't* isn't really a word or that it's slang, with the implication that slang isn't really part of the language. But paying attention to the world as it is rather than as we'd have it, we observe that, perhaps, we all use *ain't* occasionally, and some varieties of English use it quite regularly. So, from the descriptive point of view of linguistics, *ain't* IS a word.

An important facet of morphology, in particular, has to do with the spontaneous creation of words. A student once compared the rich, long, full-stressed middle vowel [i] (spelled e) in the word *anemic* to the two unstressed, anemic vowels in the first and third syllables, saying that the middle vowel is *heavy dutier* than the others. I'd never heard the expression *heavy dutier*, and I believe it passed unnoticed by the other students in the class. So, I had to interrupt the class discussion to do a quick internet search, and the results that came back assumed I'd meant to look for *heavy duties*. If the internet didn't have an attested *heavy dutier*, did that mean the student created the expression on the fly? The attested expression *heavy duty* looks rather noun-y, i.e., a noun modified by an adjective, as in *big cat*, *blue sky*, *happy camper*, but together, *heavy duty* seems to be mostly used as an adjective, as in *heavy duty boots* and *heavy duty gloves*. Now, *-er* can certainly be added to adjectives for the comparative form, as in *greener*, *taller, hungrier, happier*, but when the adjective gets to be three or more syllables, English prefers an alternative with the word *more-* of the comparative, as in *more institutional* and *more interactive*, as opposed to *\*institutionaler* and *\*interactiver*. The student, quite unintentionally, did two creative things. First, although *heavy duty* is a common enough adjectival form, she came up with, from her knowledge of English grammar, a novel form for the comparative. Second, the student did violate the general rule about English that highly prefers *more* instead of *-er* on longish adjectives. With four syllables, *hea-vy-du-ty*, we'd have expected the comparative to be *more heavy duty* or *heavier duty* rather than *heavy dutier*. Yet, despite the violation, the expression sounded natural, and, indeed, no one else in the class seemed to have recognized anything amiss about *heavy dutier*. If speakers don't react to any supposed ungrammaticality in *heavy dutier*, likely the form is grammatical – in accord with the wordformation rules of English. And if *heavy dutier* is grammatical, then, as linguists, we'll have to go back and refine our hypothesis about what the rules are for using *-er* comparatives and *more* comparatives.

We want a theory of morphology to tell us why *antidisestablishmentarianism* is constructed as it is and why it means what it means. We want a complete theory of morphology to account for all the attested words in the language. But being a scientific theory, morphology should also make predictions about what nonattested words are possible and what speakers' knowledge is for creating hitherto unattested forms like *heavy dutier*. It's the job of linguists to describe and, hopefully, explain why the student came up with *heavy dutier* not to correct her by saying *heavy dutier* isn't good English. In explaining *heavy dutier*, linguists would be adding to our understanding of the morphological rules of English.

## 1.4 Spelling Conventions and the International Phonetic Alphabet

As mentioned, linguistics is primarily interested in spoken language, not written. This is as it should be, as nearly all the languages that have ever been spoken were and are unwritten. For those few languages with written forms, the written language is a visual representation of the spoken language, but there are many differences between written and spoken language. For one, written language has commas, semicolons, apostrophes and other symbols that are lacking in spoken language. True, some punctuation reflects characteristics of spoken language, such as commas sometimes corresponding to pauses in the flow of speech or periods marking the end of a sentence. But a lot of writing language on a page involves arbitrary conventions that vary from language to language, not to mention the inconsistencies within a single language.

In other ways, too, conventional orthography in an alphabetic language, like English, doesn't reliably reflect the sounds of spoken language and, hence, the morphology. The hyphen is one problem. While the morphology literature typically uses hyphens to separate pieces within a word, standard written English uses it inconsistently for several purposes. Take the expression *quasi-* that precedes some other piece of morphology. English spelling sometimes puts a hyphen between the pieces, as in *quasi-stellar*; sometimes separates the pieces into separate written words, as in *quasi contract*; and sometimes mashes the two pieces together in an orthographically uninterrupted word, as in *quasiparticle*. Further, you'll sometimes see the same word variably hyphened, as in *quasi-stellar* and *quasistellar*. And is it *horsefly*, *horse-fly* or *horse fly*, all of which are findable on the internet? The rules for hyphenating are largely impressionistic prescriptive rules, varying from dictionary to dictionary, style manual to style manual, publisher to publisher. In the case of *quasi-*, the inconsistency in using the hyphen may well reflect speakers' and writers' unconscious confusion about the morphological status of *quasi-*, whether it's a separate word or, to some degree, part of another word. In this case, morphologists may be as uncertain as editors about how to represent the relationship between *quasi-* and the thing it's modifying.

But in principle, when morphologists use hyphens, they mean to indicate an analysis of pieces within a word. Morphologists also sometimes use the plus sign (+) and, for special cases, an equal sign (=).

As for spelling and sound, conventional orthography is problematic for presenting language data. Conventional prescriptive spelling, English spelling in particular, is a very inconsistent reflection of sounds. For example, each letter *a* in the words below is pronounced differently.

(15)  ate, father, diagram, tall

In reverse, going from sound to spelling, the sound of the vowel in *ate* has different letters across words.

(16)  ate, weigh, main, champagne, exposé, obey

And how, we may ask, are the *a*s reflecting pronunciation in the following? Each *a* is part of a letter sequence that, as a whole, represent a single sound.

(17)  ear, boat, break, breakfast, carriage

English spelling is many-to-many: one letter can represent different sounds, and a sound can be represented by different letters. In order to unambiguously reflect sound, what's required is a system in which each letter represents only one sound, and each sound is represented by only one letter.

Following conventions of presenting data in linguistics, conventional spelling will usually be used in presenting morphological data when phonological precision isn't relevant. Data from English and other languages that use some variation of the Roman alphabet will be presented in the conventional spelling of the language. Data from unwritten languages and languages that don't use the Roman alphabet are presented in a Romanized transcription based on, more or less, the International Phonetic Alphabet, to be presented below. So be aware when presentation in conventional spelling doesn't match the sound or the morphological breakup of a word. For example, the morphological analysis of the word *nationalization* is as in (18).

(18)  nation-al-ize-ation

The -*ize* is left in conventional spelling, related to the word *nationalize*, although the letter e is not pronounced in either *nationalize* or *nationalization*, and, by spelling convention, is omitted in *nationalization*.

The International Phonetic Alphabet (IPA) is a set of letters and other symbols for, ideally, representing any sound in any language with a single symbol, such that each letter symbol represents one and only one sound, and each sound is assigned one and only one letter. In principle, when linguists see a word spelled in IPA, they should be able to, at least roughly, approximate the intended sound. Square brackets are often used to indicate that IPA spelling is being used specifically for the pronounced word. Many of the IPA symbols are recognizable English letters but used in a consistent one-to-one way. Whenever you see IPA [o], always pronounce it as in the word *hope*, not as in *hot, lost*, or *move*. And if you want to refer to the last sound in *dogs*, the symbol [z] should be used.

When the text occasionally needs to refer unambiguously to a sound that the English spelling fails to accurately reflect, refer to the following lists of slightly simplified and modified IPA sound-symbol correspondences.

*Table 1.1* Simple Vowels and Diphthongs

| IPA Symbol | Conventionally spelled words with that sound |
|---|---|
| i | eat, machine, weed, equal, city, key, receive, field |
| ɪ | if, build, counterfeit, women |
| e | make, great, rain, obey, feign, cabaret |
| ɛ | bet, said, leather, many, heifer |
| æ | sat, laugh, plaid |
| a | father, bother, sergeant, heart, guard |
| ɔ | law, talk, alcohol, caught, broad, cough, bought |
| o | so, toe, sew, toad, oh, dough |
| ʊ | put, took, would, wolf |
| u | tool, rule, move, canoe, blue, blew, suit, through |
| ʌ | tub, mother, flood, double, does |
| ə | atone, easily, circus, pivot, parliament, spurious |
| ai | night, site, height, buy, sky, eye, die, dye |
| ɔi | toy, lawyer, boil, Illinois, St. Croix |
| au | pound, now, bough |

(i) Simple vowels are single vowels, while diphthongs are, in effect, combinations of vowels that are seen as a single vowel. The vowel in *cat* is simple, while the vowel in *kite* is a diphthong, effectively an /a/ and /i/ together, as suggested by the two-letter representation *ai*. Besides /ai, au, ɔi/ other English vowels such as /i/ and /e/ are sometimes described as diphthongs for reasons that don't concern us here; we'll let them pass as simple vowels.

(ii) Note that some of the above words have variant pronunciations across dialects.

(iii) Some North American dialects don't distinguish between [a] and [ɔ]; for those speakers *cot* and *caught* are both pronounced with the [a] vowel.

(iv) Sometimes identifying the letters of English spelling with the sound is arbitrary. For example, one could argue that the [u] in *rule* is represented not only with the *u* but in accompaniment with the 'silent' *e*. Whether the unpronounced *gh* in *height* is part of the preceding vowel or the following consonant is a judgment call.

Liberty is taken with the symbol r, which, in IPA, represents a trill, a rolling sound made with the tongue. The English sound in *red, stretch* and *car* (for most speakers) is actually ɹ in IPA, but we'll use the familiar r instead.

Those IPA letters will cover most of the sounds used in varieties of North American English. When presenting data from well-known European languages, the conventional spellings will be used unless precise sounds are relevant to the morphology. Less known languages are presented mostly in IPA spelling with occasional conventions of convenience used by linguists who specialize in those languages. Some additional IPA or other conventionalized alternatives used in the original data will be explained as they come up, but because something reasonably close to IPA is used for lesser known languages, you should be able to approximate the sounds of those languages as presented in the data. If you see the Persian word *miz* 'table', you should read it as rhyming with English *cheese*. Crow *bilé* 'water' is [bile], rhymes with English *bee lay*.

For more details on representing sounds in English and other languages, see the International Phonetic Association at https://www.int ernationalphoneticassociation.org/content/full-ipa-chart. An additional

*Table 1.2* Consonants

| IPA Symbol | Some conventionally spelled words with that sound |
|---|---|
| p | p<u>a</u><u>per</u>, sto<u>pp</u>ed |
| b | ta<u>b</u>, ta<u>bb</u>y, |
| t | a<u>tt</u>une, a<u>tt</u>ack, dou<u>bt</u>, ya<u>cht</u>, brou<u>ght</u>, <u>tw</u>o, walk<u>ed</u>, <u>pt</u>eranodon, <u>ct</u>enophora |
| d | <u>d</u>o, a<u>dd</u>ition, shou<u>ld</u>, mull<u>ed</u> |
| k | <u>c</u>at, <u>k</u>itty, a<u>cc</u>ount, pla<u>que</u>, li<u>qu</u>or, ta<u>ck</u>, <u>ch</u>aos |
| g | <u>g</u>one, <u>gh</u>ost, e<u>gg</u>, <u>gu</u>ard |
| f | <u>f</u>ive, ta<u>ff</u>y, rou<u>gh</u>, cal<u>f</u>, <u>ph</u>ysics |
| v | <u>v</u>isit, di<u>vv</u>y, o<u>f</u>, Ste<u>ph</u>en |
| θ | <u>th</u>ick, <u>phth</u>alin |
| ð | <u>th</u>is, ba<u>the</u> |
| s | <u>s</u>o, <u>c</u>ity, <u>sc</u>enic, mo<u>ss</u>, <u>ps</u>ychology |
| z | <u>z</u>oo, lo<u>s</u>e, fu<u>zz</u>y, <u>x</u>ylophone, Mi<u>ss</u>ouri |
| ʃ | <u>sh</u>oe, i<u>ss</u>ue, ma<u>ch</u>ine, spe<u>ci</u>al, <u>s</u>ugar, pen<u>si</u>on, mi<u>ssi</u>on, |
| ʒ | vi<u>si</u>on, trea<u>s</u>ure, a<u>z</u>ure |
| h | <u>h</u>eart, <u>wh</u>o, <u>j</u>alapeño |
| ʧ | <u>ch</u>oose, <u>c</u>ello, ba<u>tch</u>, ques<u>ti</u>on, na<u>t</u>ural |
| ʤ | <u>j</u>oin, e<u>dge</u>, e<u>x</u>aggerate, tra<u>g</u>ic, e<u>du</u>cate |
| m | <u>m</u>om, colu<u>mn</u>, tri<u>mm</u>er, cli<u>mb</u>, phle<u>gm</u> |
| n | be<u>n</u>ign, ru<u>nn</u>er, <u>kn</u>ead, <u>mn</u>emonic, <u>pn</u>eumonia |
| ŋ | si<u>ng</u> |
| r | <u>r</u>at, ho<u>rr</u>or, <u>wr</u>ite, <u>rh</u>ythm |
| l | <u>l</u>ight, ta<u>ll</u>er, is<u>l</u>e, |
| j | <u>y</u>ou, torti<u>ll</u>a, <u>u</u>se (the [j] sound is included in the letter *u*) |
| w | <u>w</u>eight, <u>wh</u>y, q<u>u</u>ack |

source with links to recordings of the sounds each letter represents can be found at InternationalPhoneticAlphabet.org.

## 1.5  Presentation of Language Data

To illustrate and describe morphological phenomena and to have evidence for general claims, language data are presented. There are a few conventions to make the presentation of data as accurate, meaningful and readable as possible. Language typically happens in streams of speech. There are pauses between sentences and phrases but, typically, not between any two or more words, which flow together in unbroken sound. So, we might present a sentence as in (19).

(19) morphologyisthegrammarofwordformation

Or even better, for phonetic accuracy, something like (20).

(20) mɔrfalədʒɪɪzðəgræmrʌvwərdfɔrmeʃn

The representation in (20) is, however, unnecessarily cumbersome. Because the focus is morphology and not phonology, conventional spelling usually suffices, unless particular points of phonetic precision are relevant. And instead of using representations like that in (19), linguists take the liberty of breaking the sentence into words with conventional spacing.

(21)   Morphology is the grammar of wordformation

Some morphologists like *wordformation* as a single written word, though you certainly could make it two written words if you so prefer or hedge your bets with a hyphen.

As mentioned, foreign language data are usually presented in the conventional spelling of the language, if that language uses a Roman alphabet; if not, the data are transcribed into IPA or an approximation of it. The data are then glossed with a roughly one-to-one translation of the meaning or function. Then a natural-sounding English translation is provided. Consider the very simple case of a single word from Persian presented in standard three-line format. Note that the data on the top line are in the Roman/IPA alphabet, as opposed to the Arabic alphabet, which is used in Persian writing.

(22)   miz      ⇐   original data
       table    ⇐   gloss
       'table'  ⇐   translation

In this simple one-word case, the translation is redundant and is included for stylistic consistency in presentation. In most cases, however, the translation on the third line is not identical to the gloss and is helpful in clarifying the intended meaning of an expression in natural English. Consider the plural form below. Although there are no morphological hyphens in speech, or in conventional spelling for that matter, a hyphen is added by the linguist to cleanly separate the two pieces of the word *miza* 'the tables' as *miz-a*. The second line, the gloss, shows a meaning or function for each piece in the data, keeping the corresponding morphological break with a hyphen. And because *table-Pl.Def* is a clunky formula (Persians don't say the equivalent of *table plural definite*), the translation is a smoother English equivalent to the Persian expression.

(23)  miz-a
      table-PL.Def
      'the tables'

As the data get more complicated, the translations are even more useful for clarity. Here's the first line of Virgil's *Aeneid*, presented as linguistic data. The macron over the *o* indicates that the vowel is long.

(24)  arm-a              vir-um-que     can-ō
      weapon-PL.Acc      man-Acc-and    sing-1.Sg.Pres
      'I sing of arms and the man'

Each word has at least two pieces, separated by hyphens, within the words. Note the *-a* ending on the noun *arma* 'weapons'. This is a single phonetic segment which, nonetheless, has at least two bits of meaning and function. First, it's a plural form, and second, it's in the accusative case, indicating that the noun is the object of the verb *canō*, 'I sing'. Because *-a* can't be further broken down morphologically, it's a complex piece, comprising both plural and the accusative. The convention is to link these two with a period in the gloss; another convention puts the relevant features in square brackets – [Plural, Accusative]. Same for the *-ō* in *canō*: it's got at least three functions, marking that the subject is first person, that the subject is singular and not plural and that the verb is in the present tense. The *-ō* could also be glossed as 'I.Pres' because the translation includes the English word *I*. In any case, the translation smooths out the clunkiness of the gloss, which might give the impression that Latin was a clunky language. Also, the translation took some liberty to translate *canō* as 'sing of' rather than merely 'sing', as the gloss suggests; "I sing arms and the man" is odd, and, besides, the translation is probably typical for this famous first line of Virgil's very long poem, though some translators insist on leaving out the preposition *of*.

Glosses are often incomplete in that the data are not fully analyzed but, rather, are simplified to focus on the points the linguist wishes to make. The analysis in the gloss in (24) is fine, but depending on how detailed the linguist wants to be and what the relevant points are, the analysis could conceivably be elaborated as in (25).

(25)  arm-a                       vir-um-que              can-ō
      weapon-PL.Acc.Neut.C2    man-Acc.Masc.C2-and    sing-1.Sg.Pres.Indic.Active
      'I sing of arms and the man'

In (25), the analysis points to the fact that the -*a*, besides indicating a plural object of the verb, also is a clue to the word being of the neuter gender of class 2 (often called the second declension). Similar for the word for 'man', which happens to be a masculine noun of the same class. The -*ō* on the verb, besides being first person, singular, present tense, is also indicative mood, used for ordinary declarative statements, and active voice as opposed to passive.

On the other hand, if the internal structure of one particular word is not a point of interest, it can be left unanalyzed, as in (26a) instead of (26b), for example.

(26a)  canō       (26b)  can-ō
       I.sing            sing-1.Sg.Pres
       'I sing'          'I sing'

Given the third-line translations, most glosses are fairly self-explanatory. A list of abbreviations used in the glosses is provided on page X.

## 1.6 Summary

Grammar is the unconscious knowledge that speakers use to produce and understand language. Morphology is the part of the grammar that accounts for wordformation – how words are analyzed into and built up from smaller pieces. By analyzing the attested words in a language, as well as by looking at how speakers invent new words, morphologists aim to articulate precisely just what speakers' morphological knowledge is.

The linguistics approach to understanding grammar is scientific, at least in spirit. Linguists observe what speakers do and don't do, describe utterances and attempt to explain the grammar underlying those utterances. In morphology – the grammar of wordformation – as in other aspects of grammar, it's no surprise that languages form words differently. Nonetheless, it will also become apparent that, despite appearances, languages do follow crosslinguistic patterns in their morphology.

## 1.7 Exercises

1. Identify the simple words and the complex words – those with more than one component piece – in the following (Over the Rainbow, n.d.).

   *Somewhere over the rainbow*
   *Way up high*
   *There's a land that I heard of*
   *Once in a lullaby*

2. Identify the simple words and the complex words – those with more than one component piece – in the first sentence of the English translation of Gabriel Garcia Márquez's *One Hundred Years of Solitude* into pieces that contribute to the meaning of the words. Comment on what the pieces add to the complex words' meanings. Some words are clearly simple, others clearly complex, but some words look like they're complex but are not.

   *Many years later as he faced the firing squad, Colonel Aureliano Buendía was to remember that distant afternoon when his father took him to discover ice.*

## 1.8 Arguable Answers to Exercises

1. We'll list the simple words without comment and then the complex words.

   *Somewhere over the rainbow*
   *Way up high*

> *There's a land that I heard of*
> *Once in a lullaby*

a. Simple words: *over*, *the* (but see *that* in the answers to Question 2), *way*, *up*, *high*, *a* (twice), *land*, *that*, *I*, *heard*, *of*, *once*, *in*, *lullaby*
b. Complex words:
   i. *somewhere*: transparently *some* plus *where*. Semantically clear, as long as we accept that *where* means 'place', on a parallel with *everywhere*.
   ii. *rainbow*: easily breakable as *rain* and *bow*. Semantically pretty clear as a metaphor of a colored bow in the sky when it rains.
   iii. *there's*: a so-called contraction of *there* and *is*. It's spelled as one word, with the apostrophe, and *-s* (pronounced [z]) attached at the end.

A few comments. The adverb *once* looks and sounds suspiciously like *one*, but abstracting *one* out of *once* leaves a semantically mysterious *-ce*, pronounced [s]. Despite the apparent *one* inside *once*, English speakers probably see *once* as a single piece. The verb *heard* is an irregular past tense, changing the vowel of *hear* from [i] to [ə], despite the constant *ea* spelling. In addition, the regular past marker *-ed* makes a surreptitious presence as *-d* in spelling, although in pronunciation, the past tense is identical to the past tense marker in, for example, *occurred*, both pronounced [d]. Still, despite some overlap between the two forms in structure, it's probably simplest to consider *heard* as a simple word that happens to have two semantic components of the verb itself along with the tense. From the point of view of a modern speaker of English, *lullaby* is surely a simple word. On a historical note, it's probably a composition of *lull* and *by(e-bye)*. This word is a good example of historical information about a word that's not morphologically obvious or relevant to the grammar of modern speakers.

2. Let's put the words in three categories: (a) unarguably simple words, (b) unarguably complex words, (c) words whose compositionality is fuzzy and, in some cases, highly abstract and conjectural.

*Many years later as he faced the firing squad, Colonel Aureliano Buendía was to remember that distant afternoon when his father took him to discover ice.*

a.  Simple words: *many, as, he, the* (but see *that* in the questionable words), *squad, Colonel, was, to, his, father, took, him, to, ice.*

b.  Complex words:
    i.  *years*: the noun *year* and the plural marker *-s*
    ii.  *later*: the adjective *late* and the comparative marker *-er*
    iii.  *faced*: the verb *face* and the past marker *-ed*
    iv.  *firing*: the verb *fire* and the *-ing* ending making the word adjectival
    v.  *afternoon*: a compound of *noon* modified by *after*, which is usually a preposition

c.  Words of questionable compositionality:
These words are most likely unanalyzable for speakers, being single units in their vocabulary. However, if you want to be overly analytical, you can make a qualified case that some of these words are complex and made of smaller units.
    i.  *Aureliano* and *Buendía*: Some proper names have recognizable parts, though it's never clear that those parts add any meaning or even if, in most cases, proper names have meaning in the same sense that common nouns have meaning. Nonetheless, someone who knows Spanish may point out that *día* means 'day' and *buen* looks like a truncated *bueno* 'good'. *Aureliano* is related to *áureo* 'golden', but does the name, therefore, really 'mean' 'golden good day'? In any case, we shouldn't assume that foreign-language morphology carries over when a word is borrowed into another language. Most often, compositional meanings of foreign words are not apparent to monolingual English speakers. On the other hand, there are plenty of word-building pieces of foreign origin that are part of English speakers' morphological knowledge, such as *anti-*, *pro-* and *-ment*. Further, carrying morphology across languages may not be as rare as has been thought (Gardani 2018).

ii. *remember*: This is almost certainly a single unit for English speakers, but the *re-* at the beginning looks suspiciously like the *re-*, meaning something like 'again', that appears in many words is recognizable, as in *rethink, repaint, rewrite* or 'back' as in *recall, retract*. But that suggests that *re-* is attaching to *member*. Of course, *member* is a word, 'person or thing that's part of a group', but that *member* has nothing to do with *remember*. Given the meaning of *remember*, a little abstraction leads to a hunch that *member* may have something to do with *memory*, but then we wonder why that *b* is in the latter but missing in the former. In fact, from an etymological perspective, *re-member* is a reasonable guess as to the makeup of the word but that kind of historical information is usually not available to speakers. Ultimately, it comes from Latin.

iii. *that*: Surely, this is a single piece, not analyzable into, say, *th-* and *-at*. Or is it? An interesting observation would be that the first sound in *that*, [ð], spelled with the two letters *th*, is the same as the initial sound in *this, those, these, the, there*, and maybe we can throw in *then* and the archaic *thither*, of variable pronunciation – [ð] or [θ] as in *thick*. Most of these words have a component of definiteness to them. However, although analyzing *th-* in this way might be of interest to a linguist, it's doubtful that speakers consider *th-* a unit of analysis, even at the unconscious level of knowledge of language.

iv. *distant*: Again, almost surely a single unit for English speakers. However, there is that *dis-* element that we saw early in the chapter. It sometimes means something like 'not', as it seems to in *disobey*, but there's also a meaning of 'apart, separate, away' as in *displace*. With any of those meanings for *dis-*, we need then to explain *tant*, and that doesn't obviously mean anything. It turns out – surprise! – that the word is, ultimately, of Latin origin, *distantia* 'distance, remoteness'. The *tant* is one of a set of related forms, including *st-, sti-, stan-* and *stant-*, which is starting to look like English *stand*. Hence, *distant* suggests 'standing away'. If that seems a stretch for English speakers, perhaps the compositionality of the word was more transparent to Latin speakers 2,000 years ago. In the end, the analysis of *distant* as a complex word may be of interest if you're fascinated by word etymologies, but it's opaque to English speakers.

v.  *when*: Surely a single unit, but it's curious that the other question words and relative pronouns start with the same *wh*, at least in spelling: *who*, *what*, *where*, *why*, not to mention archaic *whither* and *whence*.

vi. *discover*: Another example of iffy compositionality from the perspective of English, but it is a bit more transparent than *distant* if you think of *discover* as meaning 'uncover', although it admittedly takes creative leaps to get there. It's clear there are two recognizable pieces to this word – *dis-* and *cover* – but it's less than obvious how they combine to yield our meaning of *discover*. Again, we have an English word coming ultimately from Latin, this one by way of French, with historical baggage behind its meaning. Because we're on the topic of word histories, see Wootton (2015, 57–68) for an interesting discussion on the notion of discovery, various words used initially to describe it, and the gradual consensus to use *discover* and related words in European languages amid the early years of geographic exploration beyond Europe and the development of the scientific method.

# Chapter 2

# The Lexicon

## 2.1 Preliminaries

Wood, pickles, bones, water pipes, plastic bags, linguistics books. Ultimately they're all made of fundamental pieces, the chemical elements, 118 of them on last check. Stuff in the world is ultimately made of these 118 elements; combining them yields the millions of kinds of molecules that make up things such as wood, pickles and bones. Of course, the elements are further analyzable into subatomic particles, but by convention, the study of the subatomic particles is the domain of physics. Chemistry starts with the 118 elements as the basic building blocks and investigates how they combine to make up the ordinary stuff that we recognize in the world (Hambly, n.d.).

Similar to the analogy between sentence grammar and chemistry that Baker (2001) develops in *The Atoms of Language*, words can be viewed as structures built up from a set of fundamental pieces, as we saw in the discussion of *antidisestablishmentarianism* in the first chapter. But language has way more than 118 basic elements. If we're starting with the pieces that make up words, English, and presumably every language, has thousands of fundamental units, although no one knows an exact number – there probably isn't an exact, static number. The grammatical system of combining the fundamental pieces of words gives us the tens of thousands of words in any language and the capacity to make as many more as we like. As one more part of the analogy with chemistry, yes, we could further divide these fundamental pieces into individual sounds, but because individual sounds typically don't

DOI: 10.4324/9781003030188-2

have any meaning or function in themselves, these word pieces are a better place to identify the atomic elements of wordformation. These atomic units are called morphemes. What you have stored in your brain is not so much a list of words but a network of morphemes.

## 2.2 Morphemes and the Lexicon

We start with a standard presentation of what can be considered the minimal elements of meaning by offering a working definition of a **morpheme**.

(1) **Morpheme: Preliminary Definition**
     A morpheme is a minimal sound-meaning pair in language.

A morpheme links a chunk of sound to a meaning. Thus, a morpheme is not so much a thing but, rather, is a relationship, an association. The association between sound and meaning in any language is overwhelmingly arbitrary, meaning that there's no natural connection between the sounds that make up a morpheme and the meaning of the morpheme. The sound sequence in *cat*, [kæt], has nothing to do with felines, nor do the cat-denoting morphemes in other languages, such as Japanese *neko* [nɛko], Persian *gorbeh* [gɔrbɛh], French *chat* [ʃa], or Crow *kilía* [kilia]. Because the relationship between sound and meaning is arbitrary, we say, in the philosopher Peirce's terms, the sounds are symbols. Memorizing which sounds symbolize which meanings is a major task in learning any language.

The association between sound and meaning is minimal in the sense that morphemes cannot be further analyzed into meaningful pieces. The word *blackened* has three easily recognizable morphemes: *black*, *-en* and *-ed*. Starting from the left, *black* has something to do with the color; we can say that *black* denotes the color black; it's typically used as an adjective. The *-en* part takes the adjective *black* and converts it into a verb, adding the meaning of something like 'become' or 'cause to become'. Thus, *blacken* can mean 'cause to become black'. This *-en* appears in other words such as *whiten, darken, sharpen, harden, lengthen, heighten*, with the same causative meaning. Finally, now that *-en* has provided us with a verb, the *-ed* puts the verb in the past tense. Because it comprises smaller pieces in this way, *blackened*, as a whole, is clearly NOT a minimal sound-meaning pair, although each of the three pieces is. These pieces are as deep as we can go. For example, while the sound of *black* is analyzable into a sequence of sounds, the word cannot be meaningfully divided into, say, *bl* and *ack*, or *bla* and *ck*. How about *b* and *lack*? Well, *lack* IS a word, a separate morpheme, but that's not what we have inside *black*. The word *lack* has nothing to do with *black*; it's only an accident that the sound sequence in *lack* is the same as the sound sequence following the *b* in *black*. The word *black* is minimal and, therefore, a morpheme. Likewise, the *-en* and the *-ed* can't be broken up into meaningful pieces. They're morphemes, too.

Three addendums should be added here. One is that, while the sound unit is minimal, the meaning and function of that minimal unit may be complex, as shown in the following contrastive examples with variant forms of the verb *be*.

(2a) I am ready.   (2b) I was ready.   (2c) We are ready.   (2d) We were ready.
(2e) She is ready.   (2f) She was ready.   (2g) They are ready.   (2h) They were ready.

Contrasting (2a) and (2b) shows that *am* is present tense and *was* is past tense. Examples (2a) and (2c) reveal that *am* is used with singular *I* and *are* with plural *we*, while the contrast between (2a) and (2e) points to *am* being used when the subject is first person *I*, while *is* appears with third person *she*. Therefore, *am* can be translated as 'be.1.Sg.Present', with at least four bits of meaning: the verb *be*, along with three particular pieces of information: first person used with *I*, singular number and present tense. We call each of these three refinements of *be* a **feature**. Each feature specifies some semantic or grammatical information about the particular use of *am* as opposed to other forms of *be* such as *is*, *are*, *was*, *were*. Such information can be glossed as in (3), where a period separates the individual bits of meaning all present in the morpheme *am*.

(3)   am
      be.1.Sg.Pres

None of those features can be associated with any smaller part of *am*; rather, they are bundled into the morpheme *am* as a whole. Sometimes the features' bundles are represented by square brackets, i.e., [be.1.Sg.Pres].

Second, while the definition in (1) makes reference to the meaning of a morpheme, sometimes the morpheme contributes grammatical function rather than meaning per se. In the sentence below, the *that* doesn't refer to any things or events outside language. Rather, it has the language-internal grammatical function of introducing an embedded sentence, *an angel is watching over her*, i.e., a sentence within a sentence.

(4)  Irma believes [<u>that</u> an angel is watching over her].
                    ⇑
                    Introduces the embedded sentence *an angel is*
                    *watching over her*

Nor does the *-s* in *believes* have a true meaning. The *-s* is required, in the present tense, in order to have the verb 'agree' with the third-person singular subject of the verb, *Irma*. Why must the verb agree with the third person singular subject? Because English grammar says it must, at least in most varieties of the language. And why does English grammar insist on that *-s*? Because we observe that that's what speakers do. We also saw above that the *-en* in *blackened* doesn't have a semantic meaning as much as it has the function of converting *black* into a verb and adding the basic function of causation. With the point made that grammatical function is distinct from semantic meaning, it's important to recognize that there's no clean distinction between morphemes that mean and morphemes that function; in the end, it will be more accurate to talk of morphemes as being more or less semantic or grammatical. Still, perhaps most morphemes weigh in as either more or less grammatical or more or less semantic.

Thus, we can amend the preliminary definition of the word morpheme just a bit.

(5)  **Morpheme: Revised Definition**
     A morpheme is a minimal and arbitrary sound-meaning/sound-function pair in language.

Third, the sound-meaning definition of morphemes is relevant for spoken languages. Most languages are spoken, but there are also languages that pair meaning with visual signs rather than with sounds. These are sign languages, American Sign Language being one used in North America. Oversimplifying, the visual signs in a sign language comprise at least the shape, location and movement of hands, fingers and arms. It can be added that reading and writing involve the pairing of meaning with printed sequences of letters or other symbols. However, literacy is a secondary language skill, which, in contrast to spoken language, must be explicitly taught to children. Even though we'll be devoting our attention to morphology in spoken languages, for the record, let's revise the definition one more time.

(6)    **Morpheme: Rerevised Definition**
A morpheme is a minimal and arbitrary symbol-meaning/symbol-function pair; symbols are sound-based or visual-based.

Now that we have a working definition of a morpheme, let's preliminarily define what the lexicon is.

(7)    **Lexicon: Preliminary Definition**
The lexicon is the set of morphemes in a language.

*Lexicon* may seem like a fancy academic word for *dictionary*, but we'll see that a speaker's lexicon is quite different from what is found in a dictionary.

Each morpheme in the lexicon carries with it basic information somewhat like a dictionary entry does, but there are important differences between published dictionaries and speakers' mental lexicons. Consider the entry from our beloved 1987 *Random House Dictionary* for the word *vaccine*, slightly adapted.

(8)    **vaccine** (vak sēn′ or, especially British, vak′ sēn, sin), noun. **1.** any preparation used as a preventive inoculation to confer immunity against a specific disease, usually employing an innocuous form of the disease agent, as killed or weakened bacteria or viruses, to stimulate antibody production. **2.** the virus of cowpox, used in vaccination, obtained from pox vesicles of a cow or person. –Adjective. **3.** of or pertaining to vaccination **4.** of or pertaining to vaccinia. **5.** of, pertaining to, or derived from cows.
From New Latin (*variolae*) *vaccinae* cowpox (in title of E. Jenner's treatise of 1798), equivalent to vacc(a) cow + *inae*, feminine plural of *-inus -ine*.

Couldn't have said it better! How concise, how precise, how complete and succinctly articulated, and yet, how *unlike* the kind of morpheme entry you have in your mental lexicon. The dictionary is presumably factually correct in providing information that a speaker more or less knows about the word – and then some. But it's also just a little *too* articulate. If you or I were prompted to define *vaccine*, we might offer something like the following response.

(9)   Well, a vaccine is, you know, kind of a disease they inject you with, so you don't get the disease. The vaccine makes your body come up with defenses, antibodies. Your body produces antibodies that give you immunity. The vaccine makes you immune.

This definition is less articulate than what the dictionary offers, lacking some of the precision, detail and etymological information, but it probably better reflects what most speakers know about the meaning – excluding, of course, specialists better versed in what vaccines are and how they work. Nonetheless, we do have a lot of information about the word, in that we unconsciously and effortlessly access that information when hearing or using the word. Just because a speaker is pressed for an eloquent definition doesn't mean they don't know a good deal about *vaccines*.

The dictionary entry for *vaccine* does provide the North American pronunciation (/væksin/ in IPA), including where the main stress of the word is (second syllable, /sin/) and the fact that there are alternative pronunciations in British English. The entry also suggests that *vaccine* can be a noun or adjective, and there's a little addendum with etymological tidbits about the word. It was apparently coined more than two centuries ago by this Jenner person, who probably knew Latin (in those days of yore most well-educated people likely knew at least some Latin), by attaching a Latinate ending onto the Latin word for 'cow'. That might be interesting for people curious about word origins, but word history is not the kind of information most people include in the entries in their mental lexicon.

Dictionaries often are more complete and encyclopedic in their definitions than an average speaker's lexicon, and no doubt, dictionary definitions are usually factually correct. Yet they do slip up and get some information wrong, from a linguist's point of view, about what speakers know – not so much about the dates or details about word history, which speakers typically don't mirror in their lexical entries anyway, but on the grammar, something that dictionaries ought to be good at and something that speakers are keenly, if unconsciously, aware of. There's something off about the definition of *vaccine* that linguists can point to explicitly and that speakers know implicitly. Specifically, Random House gets it wrong in asserting that *vaccine* can also be an adjective. Let's look at the facts from a linguist's perspective and show that the dictionary is incorrect in reflecting what speakers know, unconsciously, of course, about the adjectival status of *vaccine* by comparing its behavior with that of other adjectives. Our argument will follow the form of the well-known Duck Argument: if it walks like a duck, it's probably a duck, and if it doesn't walk like a duck, it's probably not a duck.

The word looks like an adjective in a context like (10a), where *vaccine* occurs in the same position with, apparently, the same modifying function as other adjectives, such as *expensive* in (10b).

(10a)   The company is involved in vaccine research.
(10b)   The company is involved in expensive research.

But let's investigate further. First, nearly all adjectives have **comparative** and **superlative** variants, in either the *-er/-est* or the *more/most* forms.

(11)   fast/faster/fastest
       green/greener/greenest
       active/more active/most active

However, we don't find *vaccine* in those forms, and trying to make a comparative form of *vaccine* results in distinct oddness. If your native speaker intuitions are like mine, you'll find the sentences below unacceptable as English and, therefore, ungrammatical.

(12a)   *This compound is vacciner than that one.
(12b)   *This compound is more vaccine than that one.
(12c)   *This is the vaccinest product ever developed.
(12d)   *This is the most vaccine product ever developed.

Second, adjectives typically can be used both before a noun in so-called attributive position and after a verb such as *be* in predicative position.

(13a)   attributive *long*:   That's a long book.
(13b)   predicative *long*:   That book is long.

*Vaccine* looks like it can be used attributively (14a). but it can't be used as a predicate (14b).

(14a)   attributive *vaccine*:   The company invested millions in vaccine research.
(14b)   predicative *vaccine*:   *The company's research is vaccine.

Third, unlike nearly every adjective in English, *vaccine* can't be modified with *very*.

(15a)   That's a long book./That's a very long book.
(15b)   They've invested in vaccine research./*They've invested in very
        vaccine research.

The evidence is in: *vaccine* doesn't walk like a duck; i.e., overall, it doesn't behave like an adjective, though, of course, we'll want to explore why, in (10a), it appears to behave like one, at least in one respect. For all its precision and conciseness, the dictionary got it wrong, misstating what speakers accurately, though unconsciously, know about the word – that it's NOT an adjective! The purpose of this little digression was not to pick on the peccadillos of dictionaries; rather, it was to point out that a dictionary entry isn't the same as the entry in a speaker's lexicon, and, in this particular case, the dictionary came up short. Speakers are better informed on this point than the dictionary is. When we say that speakers are better informed about the grammar of *vaccine*'s relationship to *research* what we mean is that speakers aren't going to use the word in the sentences above marked as ungrammatical.

On the other hand, often enough, dictionary entries provide presumably correct information that speakers lack. For example, I know the word *potassium*, although I don't REALLY know what potassium is. It's a chemical element, we need it in our diets and bananas have it. Besides the pronunciation and its nouniness, that's about it. It's the stuff in bananas that we need in our diets. Not a very precise definition to say the least.

Dictionary writers make an effort to provide lots of information, even for very basic words like *dog*, again from Random House.

(16)   **dog** (dôg, dog), noun, verb, **dogged, dogging**. Noun **1.** a domesticated canid, Canis familiaris, bred in many varieties. See illustration on next page. **2.** any carnivore of the dog family Canidae, having prominent canine teeth and, in the wild state, a long and slender muzzle, a deep-chested muscular body, a bushy tail, and large erect ears. Cf canid. **3.** the male of such an animal. …

The … at the end of the entry indicates that the entry goes on and on, with 18 more uses, definitions, and idioms of *dog* as a noun. The entry goes on to include some verbal uses, including definition 23.

(17)   **23.** verb, transitive, to follow or track like a dog, especially with hostile intent, hound.

Two related words, *dogless* and *doglike*, are thrown in as part of the entry for *dog*, though they're distinct enough that they might have received separate entries. And finally, we get some etymological information about the history of the word. Overall, you and I know most of what's included in the dictionary entry, though not everything. And while the information may be in our minds somewhere so that we can use the word accurately and meaningfully in conversation, we are, typically, unable to reveal all that dictionary information so precisely and articulately.

Putting this all together, there's a lot going on in a lexical entry, the basic information about a morpheme stored in a speaker's head, but we can schematize at least the minimum amount of information. For example, at the very least *black*'s lexical entry can be presented:

(18)   black:   Phonetics: /blæk/
                Category: adjective
                Semantics: BLACK

The pronunciation is spelled in IPA, corresponding to the sounds a speaker uses to pronounce the word. The // slashes around the IPA spelling are a convention for representing the abstract stored pronunciation; when referring to the actual sounds in square pronunciation brackets are used: [blæk]. The **category**, or part of speech, is adjective. For now, we'll assume that the category is part of the lexical entry, though later we'll question that assumption. As an adjective, we automatically know something about its behavior, that it can modify nouns, as in *black cat*, *black car*. As for the semantics, we're being lazy by defining *black* as BLACK, which, at best, is circular. But the all-caps notation is simply a shortcut for indicating the meaning, the kind of color that black is, what speakers know about the meaning of *black*.

The entry in (18) contains very basic information that all speakers of English know. Of course, there's a lot of other information that speakers know, especially about the semantics and the word's association with other morphemes in the lexicon. It's a sister color of *red*, *green*, *blue*, etc. and specifically has a relation of opposite to *white*. *Black* is sometimes used metaphorically with a negative connotation, as in *a black day*, and it appears as part of a good number of words and phrases, including *blacklist*, *blackjack*, *black eye*, *black hole*, *blackout* (the noun) and *black out* (the verb). While these terms are probably separate lexical entries in a speaker's lexicon, clearly there's a relationship among them. By the way, these associations with *black* illustrate another important difference between dictionaries and mental lexicons. Despite occasional cross references between entries, dictionaries are arranged alphabetically, as a list. In contrast, a speaker's mental lexicon is more of a network of morphemes and words and their relations to each other by sound and meaning and are definitely not alphabetically arranged.

Let's look at other lexical entries relevant to a word we came across earlier, *blackened*, the *-en* and the *-ed*.

(19)  -en:   Phonetics: /ən/
             Category: suffix
             Morphosyntax: A-___ ⇒ V
             Semantics: 'cause to be'
(20)  -ed    Phonetics: /d/
             Category: suffix
             Morphosyntax: V-___ ⇒ V
             Semantics: Past tense

Note that the hyphen precedes both *-en* and *-ed*, indicating that these are suffixes. The phonetics for the first is specified as /ən/, usually pronounced simply as [n], its own syllable. The morphosyntactic information tells us that it's suffixed to an adjective and changes it into a verb. Finally, the semantics of /ən/ is causation; *black-en* means 'cause to be black'. For *-ed*, its phonetics is listed as /d/, which means it's the stored form of the morpheme, surfacing as [d] in *sway[d]*, [t] in *walk[t]* and [əd] in *host-[əd]*. The surface variations need not be listed in the lexical entry because the phonology component of the grammar makes sure that the appropriate variant is pronounced.

One more thing must be mentioned when talking about the lexicon. So far, we've defined it as the collection of morphemes, with each morpheme being a minimal sound-meaning pair. But minimal sound-meaning pairs are not restricted to single morphemes. Complex words, those involving more than one morpheme, must be listed somewhere if their meanings are not predictable from the way their components are assembled. The word *board* is minimal and, therefore, a morpheme, as is the word *black*. But what about *blackboard*? It's clearly a composition of two morphemes and, by the definition proposed, can't be in the lexicon. On the other hand, its meaning is not entirely predictable. A blackboard is not simply a board that's black. Rather, a blackboard is a largish surface of slate or similar material, affixed, typically, to a schoolroom wall to write on with chalk. Further, blackboards are sometimes green or brown, so blackness isn't essential to being a blackboard. Thus, the characteristics of a blackboard are not necessarily evident in the two morphemes *black* and *board*, which means that the relationship between *blackboard* and blackboards is, to a great degree, arbitrary and, therefore, should be in the lexicon, the place where unpredictable relationships between sound and meaning are listed. We conclude that the lexicon contains multimorphemic entries as well as monomorphemic ones.

Besides compounded words, some phrases should also be assumed to be in the lexicon if their meanings are not predictable. Such phrases include idioms, phrasal expressions whose meanings are not what they might literally indicate. *Kick the bucket* can, of course, literally mean 'kick the bucket', but the expression is usually a slangy alternative to the verb *die*. In that sense, *kick the bucket*, an idiom, while containing more than one morpheme, must be stored as a unit arbitrarily meaning *die*. Thus, idioms, too, must go in the lexicon.

(21) **Lexicon**: **Revised Definition**
    The lexicon is the network of minimal symbol-meaning/function
    pairs in a language. Included are both single morphemes and multi-
    morphemic forms whose meanings don't correspond to what we'd
    expect from the components making them up.

Some linguists opt to restrict the lexical entries to simple morphemes,
excluding complex forms, even if they're not semantically compositional, but the characterization in (21) is a good way to start. However,
it's important to be aware of the consequences of including complex
forms in the lexicon; that means that the lexicon is somehow doing
work, producing complex forms from simpler forms.

## 2.3 Kinds of Morphemes

### 2.3.1 Free and Bound

The morphemes that make up words can be classified into a number
of crosscutting groups based on which properties are being considered.
One distinction is whether the morpheme has the property of being free
or bound. A **free morpheme** is one that can stand by itself as an independent word. In contrast, a **bound morpheme** can't stand by itself
independently and appears only when attached to something else. With
some consistency, writing conventions in English and other languages
put spaces between what are ordinarily seen as separate words, but
bound morphemes are not isolated by spaces. Morphologists would
likely agree that the spacing in the opening line of Thomas Hardy's
*Far From the Madding Crowd* accurately reflects where the word
breaks are.

(22) When Farmer Oak smiled, the corners of his mouth spread till they
    were within an unimportant distance of his ears, his eyes were
    reduced to chinks, and diverging wrinkles appeared round them,
    extending upon his countenance like the rays in a rudimentary sketch
    of the rising sun.

Ignoring commas and periods, each of the space-separated sequences
of letters is a word. Words such as *when*, *till*, *they*, *an*, *round* and others

are simple, consisting of a single morpheme. Other words are complex, involving more than one morpheme, such as *corners*, *reduced* and *extending*. Analyze *corners* into its components and you get *corner* and *-s*. The morpheme *corner*, shorn of *-s*, can still be an independent word and is, thus, a free morpheme, as in (23).

(23)     "Little Jack Horner sat in the corner, eating his Christmas pie".

But the plural marker *-s*, which also appears in Hardy's *ears*, *eyes*, *chinks*, *wrinkles* and *rays*, can't stand independently. It's a bound morpheme and must attach to something, a noun in particular. Similarly, *smiled*, *appeared* and *reduced* can be broken into free *smile*, *appear* and *reduce*, on the one hand, and bound *-ed* on the other, which indicates past for *smile* and *appear* but passive in the word *reduced*. Other bound morphemes in the Hardy sentence include the *-ing* in *diverging*, *extending* and *rising*, the negative *in-* in *independent* (not to be confused with the preposition *in*, which is free*)* and a separate negative marker *un-* in *unimportant*. Depending on how analytical we are, we can lop off the *-ary* in *rudimentary* and the *-er* in *farmer* as bound morphemes.

   It's not always clear how to break words into morphemes. The word *Christmas* is interesting for making this point. Because we're a literate culture and have a history with strong influence from Christianity, we see *Christ* inside the written word *Christmas*, and maybe we guess or have been told, at some point, that the *-mas* part is a variant of *mass*. The word *Christmas* has been around a long time, appearing in Old English as *Christes mæsse* ('Christ's mass') a church mass on a certain day for Christians to celebrate Jesus's birth. However, the *Christ* in *Christmas* and *Christ* by itself are pronounced very differently: the vowel [ɪ] for the holiday and [ai] for the person; further, despite the spelling, there's no [t] in *Christmas* as we pronounce it. Finally, the *-mas* part isn't pronounced like *mass*. If not for being literate, it's unlikely speakers would perceive any morphological connection between *Christ* and *Christmas*. The point is, while we might see *Christmas* written on a page as two morphemes, it can be argued that, in spoken language, it's a single morpheme, a sequence of sounds arbitrarily connected to a certain day. It turns out that the analyzability of many words is problematic in terms of the number of morphemes involved, the boundaries between morphemes and what contribution the morphemes contribute to the overall meaning.

It's not surprising that there are complications with the idealized distinction between free and bound. First, we relied on written English for evidence that plural *-s* is a bound morpheme in that there's no space between it and the noun it attaches to. The problem is that not all languages follow the convention of spacing between words. The evidence we have from ancient inscriptions indicates that classical languages generally did not space words, at least not consistently. For example, Google the Rosetta Stone, a stele from about 200 B.C.E. with a text in Ancient Greek and two written forms of Egyptian, and you'll be hard-pressed to find spaces in the inscription. Some modern languages, too, don't bother much with spaces in their writing. Japanese, for example, does use some Western-style punctuation and does put spaces between sentences and sometimes phrases, but it typically doesn't use spaces between words. So, we have a harder time identifying bound and free morphemes in written Japanese than in written English.

Another complication, even within written English, is that it's sometimes unclear whether any given morpheme is bound or free based on whether spaces are involved. Take the Chapter 1 examples of *quasi-*, orthographically free as in (24a), orthographically bound in (24b) and orthographically quasibound in (24c).

(24a)  quasi stellar
(24b)  quasistellar
(24c)  quasi-stellar

And it's not only these examples; *quasi-* is alternatively spaced, hyphened or seamlessly attached in lots of words. While we should be careful about using written evidence for linguistic analysis, to the degree that writing conventions reflect *something* about our notions of wordhood, it appears that *quasi-*'s status is unclear with regard to being free or bound. One further set of inconsistencies is seen in words such as *blackbird*, *blackball* and *blackjack*, which are typically spelled as one word, and words such as *black birch*, *black hole* and *black eye*, which are written as two words. These so-called compound words will be discussed in Chapter 5.

Still, despite inconsistencies in the written language, speakers do have a pretty good intuition about what can be a freestanding morpheme and what must be bound to something inside a larger word. Those things we typically identify as nouns, adjectives, verbs, prepositions and some other categories of morphemes are free and can have independent status as words. These constitute, probably, tens of thousands of words. The number of bound morphemes is much smaller, but there are more of them than you might think. Some of them are listed below.

(25)   **Some bound morphemes in English**

| | |
|---|---|
| Plural -s: | *trees, bricks, conventions, squirrels, churches* |
| Possessive -s: | *Emily's cat, my daughter's laptop, the school's principal* |
| Plural possessive -s: | *the schools' teachers, the members' fees, protestors' signs* |
| Verbal agreement -s: | *The cat purrs when you rub her neck.* |
| Noun-making -s: | *economics, mathematics, physics, linguistics* |
| Progressive -ing: | *The kitty is purring; it's raining.* |
| Past -ed: | *talked, tagged, chased, emailed* |
| Noun-making -er | *talker, hunter, troublemaker* |
| Modifier pre- | *prewar, precook, pretheoretical* |
| Negative un- | *uncooperative, unintuitive, uncompromising* |
| Negative in- | *inalienable, inanimate, impossible, incoherent* |
| Location in- | *invade, implant, inseminate* |

There are a few things to reiterate about such bound morphemes. First, again, punctuation marks may or may not relate directly to morphology. Apostrophes, as in *school's* and *schools'*, are writing conventions and say nothing about the relationship of the possessive markers and the nouns they're attached to. Second, morphemes can have variant pronunciations, which may or may not be reflected in standard spelling. The phonetic differences in the pronunciation of negative *in-* are reflected in the spellings of *inanimate* and *impossible* but not in *incoherent*, in which the pronunciation of the letter *n* is [ŋ], the sound at the end of *sing*. Similarly, as we've seen in the first chapter, plural *-s* has three pronunciations: [z] in *trees*, [s] in *bricks*, which are not reflected in spelling, and [əz] in *churches*, which inserts the letter e before the s. In terms of sound, the variations are **allomorphs** of the same morpheme. In these cases, the allomorphs [z], [s] and [əz] are phonologically predictable and based on the sound that precedes them. Some allomorphs are irregular and unpredictable, such as the plural *-i* in *stimuli* and the *-a* plural in *phenomena*.

Allomorphy is common. The preposition *in* is sometimes [ɪn] but, often, in flowing speech, is reduced to a syllabic [n], in which the consonant [n] has the force of a vowel. The first vowel in *nation* is [e] but in the adjective *national* it's [æ]. Both *him* and *them* often reduce to [m] in speech, so that a sentence like *Did you see 'm?* is ambiguous between seeing one person and more than one.

A well-studied kind of allomorphy is **vowel harmony** in languages such as Turkish, Finnish and Hungarian, in which some vowels' pronunciations are affected by nearby vowels. Turkish has a plural marker with two forms, *-lar* and *-ler*, the choice depending on the vowel of the preceding syllable. Example (26), from Lewis (1967, 290), shows that the vowel [ɨ] (similar to [ɪ]) in the noun *kɨz* ('girl') prompts the *-lar* plural, while the vowel [e] in *el* ('hand') requires the *-ler* plural.

(26)  kɨz-lar    el-ler
      girl-PL    hand-PL
      'girls'    'hands'

While morphemes may have allomorphic variants, they can also sound the same as other morphemes. Two or more morphemes that sound the same are called **homonyms** or **homophones**. Homonyms are not uncommon, such as *red* and past-tense *read*, *blue* and *blew*, *eye* and *I*, the two *-er*s in *greener* ('more green') and *writer* ('one who writes'). The noun *reed* and the noun and verb *read* constitute a three-way homonym. Some four-way homonyms are *you*, *yew*, *ewe* and *U* as in *U-turn*; *bear* the animal, *bear* the verb and both adjectival and verbal *bare*; *sea*, *see* as in vision, *see* the office of a bishop and *C* as in *C-section*. In (25), there are five *-s* morphemes; a sixth is in *Let's go*, in which the *-s*, for illustration purposes here, can be considered an allomorph of *us*. In each case, there may be other homonyms that I've overlooked.

### 2.3.2 Lexical and Functional Morphemes

In principle, there's a distinction between lexical morphemes and functional morphemes. A **lexical morpheme** is one with semantic content, referring to things, events, properties and states in the world or concepts in our minds. Nouns, adjectives, verbs, adverbs and, sometimes, prepositions are good examples of lexical morphemes, such as in, respectively, *house* and *ferret*, *red* and *happy*, *run* and *think*, *fast* (also an adjective) and *there*, *in* and *above*. **Functional morphemes** have much less, if any, semantic content; their purpose is primarily grammatical in putting together words and sentences. They do, sometimes, have meaning of a sort but not in the same clear way that, for example, nouns can refer to things in the world. Among functional morphemes are those for tense, such as *-ed* in English, the infinitive verb marker *to*, such as in *To forgive is to forget* and the singular and plural markers. In Section 2.1, we saw the example of functional *that* that introduces an embedded sentence.

(27)   Irma believes that an angel is watching over her.

The *that* in (27) is a clear example of a morpheme that doesn't *mean* anything, it doesn't refer to anything in the world. It's purely language-internal grammatical purpose is to introduce the embedded clause *an angel is watching over her*.

Both lexical and functional morphemes can be free or bound. The adjective *green* is a free lexical morpheme, while *crypto-* is a bound lexical morpheme. The *that* in (27) is a free functional morpheme, while plural *-s* is a bound functional morpheme.

There's no foolproof set of properties to clearly distinguish lexical from functional morphemes, but there are some properties that each class tends to have, and each morpheme tends strongly toward one class or the other. Some morphemes have more 'semantic' content than others. Granted, the notion of semantic content isn't very clear: just how 'semantic' must the semantic content be? But nouns, verbs and adjective do tend to relate to things in the world or ideas in our minds, while functional morphemes are more grammatical and language-internal. *That* in (27) is a clear example of a morpheme with grammatical function (introducing a sentence within a sentence) but no meaning per se. On the other hand, tense, which is usually considered functional, tells us whether an event is taking place now, took place in the past or will take place in the future, and those distinctions are arguably contributing to semantic content.

A property unique to lexical morphemes as a group is that there are lots of them, while functional morphemes are much fewer in number.

For example, there are thousands of nouns in English, while the functional category of pronoun has only a handful of forms, such as *she*, *he*, *her*, *him*, *we*, *us*, etc. The verb category has thousands of members, but the category of tense boils down to three: present *-s*, and then only in the third person; past *-ed* and irregular alternatives; and future *will*. Other functional morphemes that are few in number are demonstratives, *this*, *that*, *these* and *those* and the articles *a*, *an* and *the*.

In word creation, it's relatively easy for speakers to come up with a new noun, such as *emoji*, a new verb, such as *butt-dial* or new adjective, such as *meh*. Check https://www.urbandictionary.com/ for ongoing contributions to the English lexicon, with invented forms and new meanings for old forms. In contrast, speakers simply don't willy-nilly invent new articles or tense markers or other functional words. There are exceptions to the reluctance to create new functional items. For example, while pronouns are typically considered functional items, some English speakers have been active in proposing new ones. Some of these can be found in gender neutral pronouns (https://forge-forward .org/wp-content/uploads/2020/08/gender-neutral-pronouns1.pdf).

While both lexical and functional morphemes can be short, as in *cat* and *-s*, lexical ones tend to be longer on average than functional ones. Further, functional morphemes are often phonetically reduced in speech, while lexical morphemes are less likely to undergo such reduction. For example, the numeral *two*, a lexical item, is always pronounced [tu], with a full vowel. But the functional word *to* is reducible to [t], as in *Do you want [t] go*, or it even disappears, as in *Do you wanna go*. Lexical *will* is fully pronounced in *I will you my fortune*, while the functional tense marker *will* can be contracted, as in *She'll see you at 4:30*. Another distinction is evident in language acquisition. Children's earliest words are overwhelmingly lexical, i.e., nouns, verbs and adjectives, while articles, tense markers and other functional categories come later in children's language development. Just to be clear, however, while children's acquisition of functional items such as articles and tense markers follows the acquisition of basic nouns and verbs, we continue to expand, enrich and refine our lexical vocabulary throughout our lives, long after we've mastered the basic functional items.

Two more phenomena point to a meaningful distinction between lexical and functional. One, languages are liberal about borrowing

*Table 2.1* Properties of Lexical and Functional Morphemes

| | Lexical | Functional |
|---|---|---|
| 1. | Have semantic content | Little or no semantic content |
| | Refer to things in the world | Function is language-internal |
| 2. | Nouns, adjectives, verbs and adverbs | Tense, agreement, definiteness, plural, etc. |
| | Usually prepositions | |
| 3. | Thousands of them | Few of them |
| 4. | Easy to create new ones | Very rare to add new ones |
| 5. | Can be short or long | Tend to be short |
| 6. | Usually not phonetically reducible | Often phonetically reducible |
| 7. | Acquired earlier by children | Acquired later by children |
| 8. | Very amenable to crosslinguistic borrowing | Much less amenable to crosslinguistic borrowing |
| 9. | Psycholinguistic evidence | Psycholinguistic evidence |

lexical morphemes from other languages, while grammatical things are much less amenable to crosslinguistic borrowing. In the past 1,500 years, English has borrowed thousands of words, traditionally from French, Latin, Greek and, during the eras of British and American imperialism, from dozens of other languages, but these borrowings have rarely been in the realm of grammatical function words. As an example, English has borrowed the nouns *burrito*, *taco* and *enchilada* from Spanish but not verbal endings, such as *-amos*, *-imos* and *-emos*. Finally, there is some psycholinguistic evidence of the distinction between lexical and functional, as various brain traumas and other conditions can affect the access and processing of one category but not the other. As one example, people with Broca's aphasia, among other symptoms, have great difficulty using functional morphemes such as articles, pronouns and some prepositions. Table 2.1 summarizes some properties that correlate, at least roughly, with lexical and functional morphemes, based partly on Abney (1987, 43–44).

### 2.3.3 Productive and Nonproductive Morphemes

Morphemes have varying frequency in language use. Among the most common in English are the pronouns; various forms of the verb *be*;

the articles *the* and *a*; common prepositions, such as *to*, *in* and *with*; the conjunction *and* and many frequently occurring nouns, verbs and adjectives. (Many websites have word-frequency data, including Wikipedia's Most Common Words in English.) In addition to utility in terms of how often morphemes are used, an important property is whether morphemes are used productively. **Productive morphemes** contribute to speakers' active creation of novel words, as opposed to using already existing words. When *Google* became used as a verb, sometime in the 1990s according to the Corpus of Historical American English, *-ed* and *-ing* were productively used to make the past and progressive forms of the verb. In contrast, the word ending *-th* is no longer used to make words. It does appear on perhaps a few dozen common enough English words, such as *health*, *wealth*, *truth* and *length*, but, outside a very few examples, speakers haven't been using it productively to create new words for centuries.

Productivity isn't an all-or-nothing phenomenon; rather, it's a more-or-less property that can be measured in various ways. If you scour corpora, you will find an occasional novel use of *-th* that's relatively recent, but *-th* is certainly much less productive than *-ing*. Creative wordformation will be discussed in Chapter 6, but we won't further explore ways to measure productivity here. For some discussion, see Haspelmath and Sims (2010), Chapter 6.

### 2.3.4 Roots, Stems and Affixes

#### 2.3.4.1 Roots and Stems

**Roots** carry core meanings of words and express "the basic lexical content of the word" (Payne 1997, 24). Roots, which are monomorphemic, often correspond to free nouns, verbs, adjectives, adverbs and many prepositions, but they can also be bound. Free roots include the noun *life*, the verb *sing* and the adjective *blue*. Some bound roots are *ident-*, as in *identity* and *identify*, *barbar-*, as in *barbarian* and *barbaric* and *somn-*, as in *insomnia* and *somnolent*. The roots *bio-*, as in *biology*, and *chem-*, as in *chemistry* are also bound, though they often are used independently as shortened forms of the full words as well. Roots from the lexicon are the starting point for wordformation. The root provides a **base** or **stem** for building words. We'll define a root as a stored representation that becomes a stem or base for the purposes of wordformation. To put it another way, the root is accessed and becomes a stem for the word-formation system; affixes or other stems may then be added to make words. Linguists sometimes use the notation of the square-root sign plus capital letters to indicate the root, as in √BOOK, √DRIVE, √WALK, √BARBAR, etc.

There are a good number of bound roots in English, most often of classical Latin and Greek origin and often with an academic flavor to them such as the above mentioned √BIO and √CHEM. But there are thousands of free morpheme roots that correspond to nouns, verb, adjectives and other categories of words. This contrasts with some languages in which many roots require additional morphology to be a word. The Spanish verb *hablar* is the infinitive form of 'to speak'. Removing the infinitive *-r* leaves *habla-*, which appears free in only two contexts, the third-person singular present (28a) and the imperative (28b) for giving commands. Otherwise, there's always a suffix indicating the person and number of the subject. A few of the inflected forms are in (28c).

(28a)  ella  habla      (28b)  habla!
       She   speaks.           speak.Imp
       'She speaks'.         'Speak!'
(28c)  hablas 'you speak'; hablamos 'we speak'; hablan 'they speak'.

Further, if we remove the *-a*, which indicates the *a*-class of verbs that *hablar* belongs to, we're left with the bound root *habl-*, or √HABL, which never appears in speech (except by linguists when referring to the root).

A more extreme case of bound roots that never appear in ordinary language is in Semitic languages, in which a root is a vowelless string of consonants. For example, the Arabic root √KTB, comprising three consonants, has a general meaning associated with writing and never appears by itself in speech. Depending on which vowels are interspersed where, various words with various meanings are constructed, as in the examples below (based on McCarthy 1979, 244; 1981, 374; cited in Lieber 2016; Fromkin et al. 2014, 42).

| (29a) | katab  | 'wrote'           |
| (29b) | kutib  | 'was written'     |
| (29c) | kattab | 'caused to write' |
| (29d) | kaatib | 'writer'          |
| (29e) | kitaab | 'book'            |
| (29f) | kutuub | 'books'           |

The examples in (29a–c) are verbs, while those in (29d–f) are nouns. Remove the vowels that indicate what specific noun and verb, and you're left with the $\sqrt{KTB}$ root, which, by itself, has no category. The consonant-based root is the standard analysis in languages such as Arabic, but the idea of a root without category carries over to English-like languages. Earlier, it was suggested that a lexical entry contains information about category, or part of speech. On that view, *book* is categorized as a noun. But there's also a verb form, as in *book a ticket*. There are several ways to handle the situation of the language having both a nominal *book* and a verbal *book*. One way to go is to assume that there are two entries in the lexicon: *book*<sub>Noun</sub> and *book*<sub>Verb</sub>. That assumption would multiply the number of roots in the lexicon to handle their various uses as nouns, verbs, etc.

| (30a) | drive a car/go for a drive         |
| (30b) | walk the dog/take a walk           |
| (30c) | run a mile/the home team scored a run |
| (30d) | deal the cards/a bad deal          |
| (30f) | paint the wall/roll paint on the wall |

Another view is to assume that one category is more basic and that the others are derived from it. So, for example, the entry could be *book*<sub>Noun</sub> that undergoes a conversion to *book*<sub>Verb</sub> by some morphological operation. A third theoretical option is that the root has no category, such as $\sqrt{KTB}$ in Arabic, and that the morphosyntax gives us the appropriate category. Such an approach gives us a more universal analysis to the relationship between the most basic and abstract parts of the lexicon and their forms as we actually speak. Rather than have English-like root-word relationships and Arabic-like root-word relationships, we can posit a single crosslinguistic root-word relationship.

Many morphologists lean toward a general crosslinguistic principle that roots don't have a category until they become stems and enter wordformation. But in describing words as they appear in spoken language, it's still useful to refer to morphemes designated as nouns, verbs, adjectives, etc., at least as they commonly appear in language use.

### 2.3.4.2 Affixes

Affixes are bound morphemes, excluding bound roots, that are added to stems. We've already seen affixes such as *-ed*, *-ing* and a number of *-s* morphemes. Affixes can be attached to stems in several ways. **Prefixes** are added on the left of the stem, while **suffixes** appear on the right. Below we see the negative *un-* prefix and the agreement suffix *-s*.

(31a)   un-tie
(31b)   speak-s

In Logba (32), a Niger–Congo language spoken in Ghana, the person agreement *ó-* is a prefix to the verb, roughly corresponding to the *-s* suffix in English. The word *nashína* ('everybody') is prefixed with a so-called class marker, CM, for the pronoun, telling us what class of words the pronouns belongs to. Data are from Dorvlo (2008, 31), cited in Velupillai (2012, 91).

(32)   ó-kpé        i-nashína
       3.Sg-know    CM-everybody
       'He knows everybody'.

A **circumfix** is a split affix, with both prefixal and suffixal parts. Some German perfect participles are circumfixes. The participle *gemacht* ('done') has the circumfix *ge- and -t* wrapping around the stem *mach*.

(33)   er    hat    es    nicht    **ge**-mach-**t**
       he    has    it    not      PerfP-do-PerfP
       'He didn't do it'.

Kaiowa-Guarani, an Equatorial-Tucanoan language in Brazil, circumfixes negation, $^n$*d- and -i* around the verb and other affixes (Whaley 1997, 118). The superscript $^n$ shows that the *d* has a nasal quality to it. A raised $^w$ indicates that the *g* is pronounced as in *Gwendolyn*.

(34)   ⁿ**d**-o-gʷapi-ta-**i**
       Neg-3-sit-Fut-Neg
       'He will not sit'.

Sometimes, an affix can appear as an **infix** within an otherwise undi-
vidable stem, as in the Chamorro. The infix *-um-* converts the stem into
a verb while *-in-* converts the stem into a noun (Topping 1973, cited in
Anderson 1992, 207–208).

(35)   tristi 'sad'
       tr**um**isti 'becomes sad'
       tr**in**isti 'sadness'

There are affix-like morphemes called **clitics**. These are bound like
affixes, but they have a more independent status than affixes. An
example is the pronoun-like clitic *-me* ('me') in European Portuguese
(Parkinson 1990, 275).

(36)   o      pai      deu-me      um      bolo
       the    father   gave-me     a       cake
       'Father gave me a cake'.

Prefixes and suffixes occur with stems in a linear order. We say that the
affixes and stems **concatenate**, lining up like beads on a string. Infixes
are not concatenative in the same sense because the infix intervenes
and breaks up the stem. The kind of wordformation we saw in Arabic
is also nonconcatenative, as a sequence of vowels weaves into the consonants of the root.

   Another kind of nonconcatenative morphology is found in tone languages. Tone languages, besides using consonants and vowels, also
use different pitches, or **tones**, to distinguish words. The tones are very
much like musical pitches. Sarcee, a Native American language spoken
in Canada, has three tones: high, mid and low; a high tone has a slightly
higher voice pitch than mid, which, in turn, is slightly higher than low.
The three words in (37) have the same consonants and vowels and are,
thus, distinguished from each other only by the three tones. Data are
from O'Grady et al. (2010, 41). Note that the *ł* is kind of an *l* sound, so
the three words sound something like English *mill*, but with different

pitches. While tones are often marked with diacritics above the vowels, here they're indicated with h, m, l underneath the vowel.

(37)   mił       mił       mił
        h         m         l
       'moth'    'snare'   'sleep'

The segment sequence *mił* with a high tone means 'moth', while *mił* with a mid-tone is 'snare' and low-tone *mił* means 'sleep'. The meaning of each of the three words stems from the combination of the three concatenated sound segments with the tone overlaid. The tone itself doesn't have a meaning any more than the word-initial *m* has a meaning by itself. Finally, to reiterate, the tone is not sequential or concatenative; rather, it's articulated simultaneously with the pronunciation of the vowel or syllable.

However, there are cases in which the tone is a morpheme by itself, with a specific function. When tones carry specific meanings, they are called **tonemes**, based on analogy with the word 'morpheme'. In Mono-Bili, a language spoken in Congo, tense can be marked with a tone. The sequence *da* with a high tone means past tense 'spanked', while *da* with a low tone is 'will spank'. Here we use the accent mark ´ for a high tone and ` for low tone. Data are based on O'Grady et al. (2010, 138).

(38)   dá    'spanked'    dà    'will spank'
        wó    'killed'     wò    'will kill'

We would need more data for a fuller analysis, but based on the data at hand, we might speculate that *da* by itself might mean 'spank'. Overlay *da* with a high toneme for the past tense and use a low toneme for future.

To recapitulate, tonemes are morphemes that occur on top of the sound segments, not in a sequential linear arrangement that morphemes usually occur in.

### 2.3.5 A Few Other Kinds of Morphemes

There are some chunks of sound whose semantic meanings are not as clear-cut or as easily identifiable as in most of the examples so far. In fact, sometimes, when one morpheme is removed, the remnant piece is, apparently, meaningless. In *beware* neither the meaning of *be-* nor *-ware* is immediately obvious, but we might wonder whether the *-ware* is related to *wary* and *be-* is the verb *be* in the imperative. On that analysis, we could plausibly suggest that *beware* literally means 'be wary!'. But then, in the related word *aware*, if the *-ware* is the same one as in *beware*, the *a-* lacks any obvious meaning. Some careful searching suggests that the *a-* may be the same one in *aboard*, *astern*, *atop* and *a-hunting we will go*. Historically speaking, these *a-* prefixes are likely weakened, truncated forms of *on* or *at* but that sort of historical information isn't available to speakers, except for some who may take the trouble to look them up. Generally speaking, then, this *a-* in *aware* is meaningless.

Morphemes with vague meaning are common in classical Greek and Latin borrowings or words assembled from classical morphemes. Take the supposed classical root *cap*, borrowed through various routes, tracing back, ultimately, to the Latin verb *capio*, meaning 'take, grasp, capture' and a range of extended meanings. The root shows up in English *capture*, *captive*, *captivate*, *capable*, *perception*, *recuperate*, *emancipate*, *incipient*, *except* and some others. If you've studied Latin or have taken a word-study class, the purported relationships among these words may make some sense, but only because the etymological connection has been explicitly pointed out. English speakers generally are unfamiliar with Latin and Ancient Greek and, therefore, don't see a root relationship among all those words. Because speakers' knowledge includes the meanings of morphemes, and because there isn't a very consistent meaning among the various appearances of the *cap*, it's, therefore, inaccurate to consider *cap* a true root morpheme.

In fact, there are many words that contain recognizable pieces, by either pronunciation or spelling, but that don't obviously contribute meaning to a word. These are sometimes called **ceive morphemes**. Appearing in a good number of words are pieces including *ceive* (which, actually, happens to be Latin *cap* transmogrified through French), such as *deceive*, *perceive*, *receive* and *conceive*. Each is analyzable into recognizable pieces: *de-ceive*, *per-ceive*, *re-ceive* and *con-ceive*, but in none of these words can we attribute a specific meaning to any of the parts. Lieber (2016, 47), citing Bauer et al. (2013) calls these **formatives**, elements whose forms are recognizable and seem like morphemes but whose meaning is unclear, inconsistent or nonexistent.

Similar to formatives are **cran morphemes**, so named from the word *cranberry*. As in the case of formatives, we end up with at least one piece of a word that doesn't mean anything; we know what *berry* means but not *cran-*. Unlike formatives, cran morphemes have a very restricted, often unique, appearance in the language. Until recently, *cran-* only appeared in the word *cranberry*, but has become somewhat productive thanks to the marketing wonders of selling an unending variety of juice mixes. According to one analysis, going back to a pre-English Germanic ancestor language, *cran-* is the word *crane*. For whatever reason, the berries were associated with the bird, and they were christened *crane-berries*. But the modern pronunciation [kræn] leaves the relationship to *crane*, pronounced [kren], opaque at best. Speaking of berries, *huckle-* and *mul-* are two more cran morphemes: we know what huckleberries and mulberries are, but what's a huckle, what's a mul? The days of the week give us *tues-*, *wednes-*, *thurs-*, *fri-*; perhaps many people know that these refer to Norse gods. You may or may not know, despite the difference in pronunciation, that *Monday* [mʌnde] is for the moon [mun] and that *Saturday* honors the gloomy Roman god Saturn. The only name for a day that's eminently transparent is *Sunday*. The first part of *lukewarm* used to mean 'tepid' but has since otherwise dropped out of use, now only hanging on as an essentially meaningless appendage to *warm*.

**Phonesthemes** are another category of word part that aren't quite run-of-the-mill morphemes. However, at least a general association can be attributed to them, if not a meaning per se, so maybe they just pass the meaning criterion for being a morpheme. But minus the phonestheme itself, the remainder of the word is opaque at best. For example, we can observe, or at least infer, a meaning of shining, sparkling or brightness in some words that begin with *gl-*:

(39)      glare, gleam, glimmer, glint, glisten, glitter, glow

But take off the *gl-* and we're left with the following bits that make no contribution to the semantics of the words.

(39)   -are, -eam, -immer, -int, -isten, -itter, -ow

Perhaps *gl-* is a remnant of a fuller form in an earlier historical stage of English, but that still leaves the meaningless stuff that follows. Other words that might have the same *gl-* are *glass*, *glance* and *gloam*. Here are a few other candidates for phonestheme status.

(40a)   sn-    snout, snarl, snicker, sneer, sneeze, snot
(40b)   spl-   split, splint, splinter, splay, splice, splash, splotch
(40c)   sl-    slide, slick, slid, slip(pery), slime
(40d)   sp-    spatter, spit, sputter, sputum, spew, spark
(40e)   squ-   squeeze, squelch, squat, squint, squish, squash, squirt
(40f)   -le    sparkle, spittle, icicle, nipple, puddle, manacle, tinkle

**Extenders**
Often enough, there are other hard-to-explain bits popping up in words, without apparent meaning and without regular phonological patterns. The bound root *gyn-* has something to do with women and *-ology* means 'the study of'. We know that the meanings of complex words aren't a literal composition of their parts, so the fact that *gynecology* doesn't mean 'the study of women' isn't particularly surprising. What is mysterious is the *-ec-* in the middle of the word. This sort of piece is sometimes called an **extender** or **root extender**. Etymologists will point out that roots are sometimes borrowed in multiple forms from another language, and here, the variant Greek sources might have been simple *gyn-* and *gunaik-*, the latter accounting for the *-ec-* piece in *gynecology*. Above, we saw that *cap-/cep-/cip-/cup-* were variant forms of the Latin *capio* and its derivatives, borrowed independently either directly from Latin or through French or another language. From the modern English speaker's point of view, however, *-ec-* simply extends the root.

## 2.4 Summary

As speakers, we have access to a network of morphemes, the building blocks of words and, ultimately, sentences. Morphemes come in different types, lexical and functional, roots and affixes, productive and unproductive morphemes, for example. Each morpheme's entry in the lexicon has information about its meaning, function, pronunciation and how it combines with other morphemes. Languages differ in how much and what kinds of morphemes are available for wordformation.

## 2.5 Exercises

1. Quiché morphemes. Quiché, also known as K'iche', is a Mayan language spoken in Guatemala. Look at the following data from Mondloch (1978, 111–112). The data are adapted and somewhat simplified for the forms of the words and their meanings. Given the meanings of the words, look for which morphemes appear with which meanings. What is the consistent morpheme for the basic verb that appears in all the examples? What morpheme occurs for the present tense? For the past tense? For each of the pronouns 'I', 'you', etc.?

   List the morphemes and their translations and describe the linear order of the morphemes in the Quiché verb.

   i.    cimmesonic   'I sweep'.
   ii.   catmesonic   'You sg. sweep'.
   iii.  camesonic    'He sweeps'.
   iv.   cujmesonic   'We sweep'.
   v.    cixmesonic   'You pl. sweep'.
   vi.   cemesonic    'They sweep'.
   vii.  ximmesonic   'I swept'.
   viii. xatmesonic   'You sg. swept'.
   ix.   xmesonic     'He swept'.
   x.    xujmesonic   'We swept'.
   xi.   xixmesonic   'You pl. swept'.
   xii.  xemesonic    'They swept'.

2. Explain whether the morphemes in Question 1 are free or bound.

## 2.6 Arguable Answers to Exercises

1. All the words have to do with sweeping, varying in who's doing the sweeping when. What's constant in all the words is *mesonic*. We hypothesize that *mesonic* means 'sweep'. We'll call this the stem of all the forms.

Note that all the present forms (i–vi) begin with *c-* and that all the past forms (vii–xii) begin with *x-*. We, therefore, conjecture that *c-* is a prefix indicating present tense and that *x-* is for past tense (vii–xii).

Between the tense prefixes and the *mesonic* stem are morphemes that correspond to who's doing the sweeping: the subject. Examples (i) and (vii) have *im-* for first person singular, corresponding to English 'I'. The prefix *at-* appears in (ii) and (viii) for second -person singular. Examples (iv) and (x) host *uj-* for first-person plural 'we', while *ix-* indicates second-person plural. When the subject is 'they', third-person plural, an *e-* appears, as in (vi) and (xii). So far, everything fits into nice patterns. The one inconsistency is the morpheme for third-person singular in (iii) and (ix). When the verb is present tense, *a-* pops up for third-person singular, but in the past tense, there's nothing between the *x-* past tense prefix and the stem *mesonic*. Thus, we'll use the notation Ø- for third person 'he' in the past.

We, thus, have the following morphemes.

| Category | Morpheme | Meaning |
|----------|----------|---------|
| Stem     | *mesonic* | 'sweep' |
| Prefix   | *c-*      | Present |
| Prefix   | *x-*      | Past |
| Prefix   | *im-*     | 1.Sg |
| Prefix   | *at-*     | 2.Sg |
| Prefix   | *a-*      | 3.Sg in the present |
| Prefix   | *uj-*     | 1.PL |
| Prefix   | *ix-*     | 2.PL |
| Prefix   | Ø-        | 3.PL in the past |

As for ordering, the verb is constructed as Tense–Person/Number–Stem.

That's what the data tell us so far. Further data of other verb forms will inform on a finer-grained analysis. For example, further data would show that the *c* at the end of the stem is an independent piece with a specific contribution and should, therefore, be extracted from the stem we've posited so far. But we can't know that from the limited data so far.

2. In the limited data presented, no morpheme ever stands alone, so we propose that *mesonic* is a bound stem requiring tenses and subject prefixes that, in turn, require a stem to be attached to. Also note that, based on the translations, each of the Quiché verbs corresponds to a sentence.

# Chapter 3

# What They Are and Where They Come From

## 3.1 Preliminaries

My tenth-grade English teacher constantly reminding us students of his massive intelligence, boasted that his vocabulary was "somewhere in the neighborhood of 100,000 words". He didn't explain how he arrived at that number, though he may have used something like the convenient method described below in Section 3.3 for estimating vocabulary size by sampling a dictionary. Whatever the method, we students accepted the stereotype that having a large vocabulary is a sign of intelligence and that our teacher's vocabulary was larger than ours. Little did we know that our own adolescent tenth-grade vocabularies weren't too shabby either and nothing to shake a stick at.

How many words do you know? How many words are there in English? Where do all those words come from? The first two questions, obviously related, are impossible to answer with any precision, but taking a stab at answering them, nonetheless, reveals something important about the size of a language's lexicon. The third question is a tangent from morphology per se, asking and briefly answering how those words got into our brains as part of our language facility.

## 3.2 What's a Word?

Though we've posited that the minimal units of meaning in a language are morphemes rather than words, for convenience, we'll work at the

DOI: 10.4324/9781003030188-3

level of words in estimating vocabulary size, as most people think of vocabulary size as how many words they know. Still, we need to be precise, and in order to calculate the number of words someone knows, we'd better have a definition of what it is that we're trying to count. At the beginning of Section 1.2, morphology is defined as the grammar of words, but we weren't precise about defining what a word is, and throughout the first two chapters, it was demonstrated that, whatever words are, many of them are decomposable into smaller pieces – morphemes. Thus, a better estimate of vocabulary size would entail counting the number of known morphemes. However, in the method we'll propose for estimating the size of the lexicon, the English lexicon in particular, dictionaries are very useful for arriving at an estimate, and conventional dictionaries are much more about words than morphemes, so we'll rely on intuitive notions about what words are and count them instead of morphemes. Still, we should explore why defining what words are is so difficult.

Full disclosure: no one knows what a word is. There is, so far, no definition that covers all the things that linguists identify as words in all languages. Even within a single language, it's not always clear whether a particular sequence of morphemes is a single word or more than one. This was illustrated in Section 2.3.1, where it was suggested that the variant spellings of *quasi stellar*, *quasistellar* and *quasi-stellar*, with or without a space or hyphen, might reflect speakers' collective indecision about whether *quasi* is a word or a bound morpheme, or both depending on context. Other reasons to doubt spacing and other orthographic conventions as reliable indicators of wordhood include the fact that not all written languages use spaces in the same way. In any case, linguistics focuses on spoken language, not written, and certainly in speaking, speakers, typically, do not pause between words, though they may pause between larger units such as phrases and sentences. Further, the vast majority of languages that have been spoken over the hundreds of thousands of years humans have been wandering the globe have been unwritten. Those languages have words as well but have left no written clues as to how speakers might have chosen to break up the flow speech sounds into words and phrases. Finally, according to some morphological theories, words are, at best, a convenient reference point between morphemes and sentences. It's certainly intuitive for us, as linguists and as ordinary speakers, to refer to words, but it may be that the level of words is a convenient fiction. And there we are, in the troubling position of being in a field dedicated to the structure of words when we're not really sure what words are. Nonetheless, we'll provide a working definition, which, at least, is intuitive if not theoretically rigorous, and which, we hope, will, at least, get us in the ballpark of an answer to questions about vocabulary size.

(1)   **Word: Preliminary Working Definition**

A word is one or more morphemes that can stand alone in ordinary language use.

We're looking for short expressions that are potentially words, and one way to get short expressions is to prompt them with questions. If someone asks, '*How many cardinals did you see?*', the answer might be *three*. According to the definition in (1) *three*, as an answer, is evidence that it's an independent word, which also happens to be a single morpheme. If the question is '*What kind of birds did you see in the park this afternoon?*', an answer might be, '*Cardinals*', all by itself. Thus, *cardinals* is a word, which happens to be two morphemes, *cardinal* and *-s*. The *-s* is not a word because we never hear plural *-s* by itself, unless a morphologist is talking. Note the appearance of the word *ordinary* in the definition. Of course *-s* can be an answer to the question '*What is the regular plural marker in English?*', but, in this case, we're 'mentioning' the *-s*, not actually 'using' it in ordinary language.

However, an answer to the question '*What did you see in the park this afternoon?*' could also be '*Three cardinals*', which, although three morphemes, is a standalone answer. Our intuition, however, is that *three cardinals* is two words, not one. We need to tweak the definition in (1) just a bit to get closer to what we think a word is. It's still not foolproof, but we'll go with it.

(2)   **Word: Revised Working Definition**

A word is one or more morphemes that can minimally stand alone in ordinary language use.

While *three cardinals* can stand alone, we can find within that expression more minimal parts that can stand alone, *cardinals* and *three*. In that sense, *three cardinals* isn't minimal. So, both *cardinals* and *three* are words, but *three cardinals* is something larger than a word.

Further analyzing *cardinals*, it's natural to think that *cardinal* by itself is a word, although it's a little harder to get it to stand alone in English because singular count nouns tend to occur with determiners such as *the*, *a*, *this* or *that*. But perhaps we can get around this general rule with special conversational context. Consider two birdwatchers on the edge of a wood when a brilliant red male cardinal flies by. '*What was that?*', asks one birdwatcher. '*Cardinal!*', answers the other. So *cardinal* is a word. Even more difficult is to find a context in which a word like *the* or *a* stand alone in ordinary language. True, if someone asks, '*What's the definite article in English?*', the answer could be '*the*', but that's another example of mentioning something about the language rather than using the language in ordinary speech.

There are other word-identification tests that might help us with *a* and *the*, which we certainly feel are independent words. Can you insert other words like adjectives between two morphemes? If you can, you probably started with two words; if not, you probably started with two morphemes in a single word. Back to *the*. Although it doesn't appear by itself in ordinary language use, the adjective *red*, which is a word on the single-word-answer test ('*What color is that bird?*' '*Red!*'), CAN appear between *the* and a noun like *cardinal*: *the red cardinal*. In fact, based on an expression like *the big, bright, chirpy, red, male cardinal*, it seems that any number of adjectives can appear between *the* and the noun, so we have evidence by another test that *the* is a word. In contrast, no adjectives can separate *cardinal* and *-s*, providing further evidence that *-s* isn't a word.

The definition in (2) will turn out to have weaknesses, but it serves well enough for our purposes.

## 3.3 So, How Many Words?

To estimate how many words there are in English and how many words any given speaker knows, we need a large collection of words, and a convenient source is dictionaries. What we'll do is take a sample of all the entries in a dictionary and see how many entries in the sample you know. Dictionaries will usually boast how many entries they have, so we'll use the advertised entry count as the number of words in the dictionary. We'll guess that a large dictionary will have most of the attested words and is, thus, a reflection of the number of words in the language. But first, there are a few cautions about equating the number of dictionary entries with the number of words in the language.

According to the Wikipedia article *List of dictionaries by number of words*, the *Oxford Dictionary* has more than 600,000 wordforms, including 47,000 obsolete words. On the one hand, large dictionaries like Oxford and Random House inflate, certainly with some linguistic as well as marketing justification, their number of entries by including idioms and other multiword expressions, along with a lot of proper names such as *Commerce*, a town in southwest California, and the names of famous people. On the other hand, dictionaries undercut the number of entries by lumping together words of the same form that really should be separate entries. For example, the verb *run* in *run a company* is not at all the same word as in *run a program, run a marathon, the river runs north, the Yankees scored three runs in the first inning* or *there's a run in my stocking*. It would be more precise to consider all these different *run*s as separate words with distinct meanings and not just variations of a basic meaning of the same word.

Also, a dictionary is inconsistent in whether it lists various derived and inflected forms. On the one hand, Random House compiles accompanying lists of attested words with the same prefix; in these lists, no definitions are provided with the words because the words are semantically transparent. If you know the meaning of *apply*, you also know the meaning of *reapply*, so dictionaries, understandably, find no need to provide a separate entry for *reapply*. Random House lists 500-some attested words that start with *pro-*; nearly all the *pro-* words, pretty transparently, mean 'for, in support of' something. This is similar for words starting with prefixes such as *de-, hyper-, inter-, multi-, non-, out-, pre-, re-, sub-, super-, un-* and others. All these lists of prefixed words cumulatively add thousands of words to Random House's number count. On the other hand, the dictionary doesn't provide similar lists for attested words built with suffixes. The suffix *-less* gets its own

entry as a bound morpheme, and some *-less* words get their own list-
ing, such as *penniless* and *heartless*, but we don't get an extensive list
of attested words that end with the *-less* morpheme. Same for *-al, -er,
-ish, -like, -ment, -ness* and many other suffixes. This is all getting
quite complex, so let's simplify and guess that the overcounts and the
undercounts roughly cancel each other out. Then we'll simply go with
Random House's advertised count of 315,000 entries, which we'll
then simplify and interpret as 315,000 words. Finally, just to qualify,
yet again, that number may be conservative, as some claims put the
English vocabulary at 500,000 words or more. You are free to object to
the proposed methodology and assumptions, but at least we're trying
to be clear about what the method and assumptions are.

To get a handle on the number of words in *your* lexicon, all you
need to do is take a random sample of the dictionary entries, say the
third entry on every twentieth page, and keep a record of how many of
them you know. Let's overlook the problem of what it means to *know*
a word; as we saw in the first chapter, there are plenty of words one
might claim to know, although your understanding of any particular
word ranges from clarity and precision to vague awareness. So, going
by a gut feeling about whether you know a word, calculate what percentage of those sample words you know and multiply that percentage
by 315,000. There are 2,214 pages of entries in Random House. Find
the third entry on every fifth page, giving you about 443 entries. If
you know 49 of the sample words, that's about 11% of them. Then,
assuming that the sample is representative of the whole dictionary, you
extrapolate that you know 11% of 315,000 entries, or about 34,650
words. Of course, that total might well include entries of names of people, famous events, things that aren't really words. Still, the estimate
is informative, telling us *something* about the size of your vocabulary.
For one, it surprises many people, including some of my students in
linguistics classes, who sometimes vastly underestimate how many
words they know. When I throw out the question to students in both
undergraduate and graduate classes, it's not uncommon for them to
guess vocabularies of as small as 1,000 words. Your vocabulary is
greater than you might think!

A vocabulary of more than 34,000 words sounds impressive, but
compared to what? It's in the ballpark of the 30,000-plus words that

Shakespeare is estimated to have used in his written work, though he certainly knew many more that never made it into his poems and plays. In fact, Efron and Thisted (1976) estimated that Shakespeare's vocabulary was more than double the word count in his works. The Bard aside, there have been many attempts to calculate people's vocabulary. In one recent study, it was estimated that an average 20-year-old college student knows 42,000 'lemmas' (*cat* and *cats* are a single lemma, as are *walk*, *walks*, *walked* and *walking*) along with another 4,200 multiword expressions whose meanings aren't obvious from the components of the expression (Brysbaert et al. 2016). A number of other calculations, depending a lot on how the counts are done, vary from 45,000ish for high school graduates to more than 60,000 for individuals who might read a lot (Bloom 2000, 6). Pustejovsky and Batiukova (2019, 3) hazard that a speaker might know up to 250,000 'lexical entries', including both active and passive vocabulary and some 20,000 compound forms and maybe 200,000 or more proper names.

It's important to remind that your lexicon is more than words. More generally, the lexicon contains morphemes. In Section 2.3.1, it was explained that some morphemes are bound, needing to be attached to a stem and, thus, not independent words. Examples are past *-ed*, plural *-s*, negatives *un-*, *a-* and *non-* and roots such as *tele-*, *micro-* and *octo-*. Dictionaries do list some of these bound forms but not all. How many of these bound forms should we tabulate as part of the lexicon? It's hard to say, but Sloat and Taylor (1992) list nearly 74 pages of these bound forms, what they call "base forms". Estimating about 20 forms per page, that gives us nearly 1,500 additional morphemes as part of our lexicon.

It's not surprising that any one speaker's lexicon is smaller than the entire lexicon of the language for all speakers. Speakers may share thousands of commonly used words, but many words to be found in a dictionary are used primarily in restricted contexts: technical terms for specialized fields of science, business, engineering, sports, literary terms, slang terms that not everyone knows, vocabulary that may be used in one dialect of English but not others, etc. Because English has written records going back more than a thousand years, a large dictionary is also inflated with words that no one uses anymore but that do appear in older texts. If English didn't have a long, written history, such words would have long been forgotten.

## 3.4 The Source of the Lexicon

### 3.4.1 Early and Later Acquisition

Where are these words, and how did they get there? Obviously, they're stored in your brain as part of your language knowledge and related to your knowledge about the world. Research in **psycholinguistics**, which studies the interaction between language and psychological processing, provides some information about how words are stored and accessed, but little is known about where any particular word is stored or precisely how it's accessed. One fundamental finding, which shouldn't be surprising, is that, unlike the alphabetically arranged words in a dictionary, the words in a speaker's lexicon are arranged in a complex network related to each other by meaning, grammar and sound. **Priming experiments** show that when one word is activated other related words are activated as well. For example, in controlled conditions, if a researcher asks you for an English word you might say anything. But if the researcher primes or prompts you with the word *cat* and then asks you to respond with the first word that comes into your head, you're very likely to say *dog*, or maybe, less likely, *pet* or *mouse*. Such experiments are typically done not with a single speaker but with large numbers of speakers in order to observe general patterns among speakers. Thus, if the researcher asks 100 test participants to respond to *cat*, and most of them respond with *dog* and no one responds with *astronaut*, for example, then we conclude that *cat* and *dog* have a closer relationship in the lexical network than *cat* and *astronaut*. And even if one or two people do respond with *astronaut*, the time it takes to get to that word under the prompt of *cat* is much longer than it takes to get to *dog*. Clearly, the words *cat* and *dog* have a close semantic relationship in the lexical network. Psycholinguistics is a fascinating field of study. A very accessible and informative book about how words are mentally organized is Jean Aitchison's *Words in the Mind*.

How did those words get into your head? When we're still wobbling in Mom's womb, we're being exposed to language as sound input, particularly from Mom's voice sending reverberations through her body. By about 18 weeks, babies *in utero* can hear things, including their mothers' voices, and soon after birth, babies recognize and prefer their mothers' voices over other female voices, a result of the baby being familiarized with it in the womb. But more to the point with regard to the lexicon and morphology, prenatal and postnatal children are exposed to language very early on, as they begin the process of language acquisition. From the moment of birth, infants are bombarded with language input from parents, siblings, other family and members of the community. *Input* is the operative word here because, given a sufficient amount of input from language being used around them, children will figure out the meanings of words along with the grammar of the language they're exposed to in six or seven years, without much in the way of explicit instruction.

With a good amount of variation, children utter their first words with some sort of phonetic and semantic consistency around the age of 1, but they've been developing a passive vocabulary, words they understand but might not produce, well before that. Many studies have attempted to measure children's passive and active vocabularies. For example, Fenson et al. (1993, cited in Barrett 1995, 362) estimated that, on average, 13-month-old children are able to produce 10 words and comprehend more than 100 words. This imbalance between active and passive vocabulary holds through life, which is to say that, even as adults, we passively recognize many more words than we actively produce in conversations. In any case, word learning proceeds through the lifetime, with various spurts at different ages and a flattening in later adulthood. Bloom (2000, 35–45) calculated that children from 12 to 16 months old add about 0.3 words each day, increasing that rate to 1.6 words per day by the third year. Between 6 and 8 years of age, according to Bloom, children might be adding 6.6 words a day, with that number jumping to more than 12 words per day between 8 and 10 years of age! That kind of vocabulary expansion is an impressive achievement; if you've tried learning a language as an adult, you can appreciate how difficult it is to learn a dozen new words a day, every day, and remember them all.

By some measures, peak learning spreads through the ages 10 to 17. Much of the vocabulary acquisition is what children pick up from the community they interact with: parents and siblings, other family, neighbors and playmates, teachers, television, videos and social media, not to mention reading skills in general. Some studies have estimated that schoolchildren are exposed to 100,000 different word meanings, including 85,000 word roots (Clark 1995, 393). We're constantly adding new words through our interactions with others, our jobs and fields of specialty, interests, technology, culture, etc. Brysbaert et al. (2016) suggest that, between the ages of 20 and 60, an average speaker adds a new word to their lexicon every couple of days. Maybe we don't remember them all, but this constant learning reflects the fact that the lexicon is dynamic, not merely a static list of words.

### 3.4.2 Transmission across Generations

Children learn words from the people they interact with in their various social communities. But where did those people get their words? Pretty much the same way: learning vocabulary as children learning the language from those around them, adding to their vocabulary throughout their lives. Stated simply, each generation of speakers gets their vocabulary from the previous generation of speakers. Of course, any generation will alter some words that have been handed down to them and come up with some new words and drop others, but the vast majority of the words are pretty much the same across the time of a single generation.

If each generation is getting its lexicon from the preceding generation, we can surmise that the lexicon used by speakers today, ultimately, has its source in the distant past. Over time, some words fall out of use or change their pronunciation and meaning as part of the natural process of language change, but plenty of words maintain enough phonetic and semantic integrity as they're passed down through the generations that they are evidence of parts of the lexicon continuing through the generations for hundreds and thousands of years. With this kind of transmission of words across time, we've bumped into the domain of historical linguistics.

**Historical linguistics** traces the history of languages and how they change over time. A crucially important tool for historical linguists is **comparative linguistics**, in which similarities among languages are analyzed in order to work back through changes in each language to arrive at ancestor languages from which they sprang. It's common knowledge that the modern Romance languages, such as Italian, Portuguese, Spanish, French and Romanian (and let's not forget all the regional and social variants of those languages!), sprouted from the same mother language: Latin. Over 2,000 years, the speakers of what were once dialectal varieties of Latin lost immediate contact with each other; the varieties of the language they spoke underwent independent changes, eventually becoming the separate Romance languages of today. In the case of the Romance languages, there are written records of older forms of these languages and their Latin ancestor. Most often, however, older forms of languages are unwritten, and the comparative method yields hypothesized ancestral forms – best guesses about the phonetic forms and semantic meanings of the ancestral words without the luxury of written sources of older forms of languages to compare to.

A key strategy in comparative linguistics for working back toward an ancestor language is to look for systematic similarities among the daughter languages. The words may not be exactly the same, but they have enough in common phonetically and semantically to eliminate the possibility that the similarities are simply accidents. Words can also be similar across languages because of contact among their respective speakers. That is, a language can 'borrow' words from other languages, and, in fact, such borrowing is very common. English hosts thousands of words that it took from other languages, especially French of the Middle Ages in the aftermath of the Norman invasion of England in 1066. But after sifting out the borrowings, we're still left with enough words in one language similar to words in other languages to suspect that the similarities are due to the languages having evolved from a common ancestor. A simple example will illustrate how we can trace back to indicate that one word has been around for thousands of years.

The English word for 'female parent', *mother*, has **cognates**, words similar in sound and meaning, in many languages. The following are a few, in the standard spellings of each language, except for Persian, which is transliterated from the Arabic alphabet.

(3)  **Words for *Mother* in Some Languages**

| | |
|---|---|
| English: | mother |
| German: | Mutter |
| Dutch: | moeder |
| Icelandic: | móðir |
| Spanish: | madre |
| Italian: | madre |
| Persian: | madær |

The words all begin with the letter m, representing the sound [m], and all have a t, d, th or ð in the middle (the sounds [t], [d] and [ð]) and an r in the second syllable. By considering what sorts of changes are common, historical linguists have hypothesized that the mother language's consonants for this word were \*m, \*t and \*r, the asterisks indicating reconstructions, or hypothesized protoforms. The ancestral vowels are more complicated to work out, but one guess is that they might have been \*a and \*e. Putting it all together, the mother word for *mother* is reconstructed as \*mater. One note of caution: the reconstruction of \*mater illustrated here is based on only seven languages. The actual and more thorough reconstruction is based on 'mother' words from scores of modern and older languages, including the Slavic languages, Greek, Hindi and many more.

It should be noted that not all reconstructions are as transparent as the relationship between *mother* and \*mater. The cognate cousins of the English word *wheel* include Latin *colere*, which, in turn, shows up borrowed into English in words like *cultivate*; Greek *kuklos* 'circle, wheel', showing up in borrowed form in our word *bicycle*; Sanskrit *cakra*, borrowed as *chakra* in English, referring to one of the supposed seven wheels of energy in the body; Modern Persian *dočarxe* 'bicycle'; along with a host of even more obscure forms in various Indo-European languages. Taken together, the hypothesized protoform of these words is \*kwel. Over the past two centuries, historical linguists have carefully worked with cognates from dozens of languages in Europe and Asia to reconstruct hundreds of words in the ancestor language.

Historical linguists have posited that the ancestral language, whose lexicon included \*mater and \*kwel, called **Proto-Indo-European**, might have been spoken some 6,000 years ago, give or take, perhaps somewhere near the Caspian Sea. Technical linguistic and anthropological details aside, the take-home point for morphology is that hundreds of hypothesized words, such as *mater and *kwel, have been passed down in modified forms through hundreds of generations to modern speakers of English, Dutch, Persian, Hindi and many other **Indo-European** languages spoken in Europe, Iran and nearby areas, as well as Pakistan and most of northern India. Since the European colonial era starting around 1500, Indo-European languages have, of course, spread to the Americas, Australia and New Zealand, parts of Africa at the expense, often deliberately and perniciously, of indigenous languages in those areas. For information and maps of where Indo-European languages are spoken, see the Wikipedia article *Indo-European Languages* listed in the bibliography. Also see *Language Family*, also a Wikipedia article, for a look at the geographic distribution of Indo-European and other language families.

## 3.5 What's in the Lexicon

The lexicon is a network of thousands of morphemes that we put together to make words and sentences. The morphemes come with different categories, functions and meanings used in different ways to assemble those words and sentences. Here, we look briefly at the some of common kinds of morphemes in a language's lexicon. Some of these morphemes will come up in more detail in subsequent chapters, so, here, we just take a whirlwind tour. Some morpheme types are common across languages, and some may be universal, meaning that there's some evidence that all languages have them. For example, Baker (2003) argues that verbs, nouns and adjectives are available in all languages. Among other crosslinguistically common morpheme types are pronouns corresponding to the English words *she* and *he* and demonstrative words such as *this* and *that*. But also see sources in Rijkhoff (2000, 217) for opposing views that even these seemingly basic categories might not be universal.

Even if nouns, verbs and adjectives are universal, some of the other categories mentioned below clearly are not; some languages have them, and some don't. But even if some word categories are absent in some languages, it's still important to note when a category appears in *most* languages or, in contrast, very few languages because the frequency of appearance of word types across languages can suggest something important about the nature of human language in general. One more thing to note is that even if a language lacks a particular word type, that language's ability to express ideas is not compromised because there are other means to get any intended message across. For example, a language may lack a dedicated morpheme for making nouns plural, but either context or some other options of expression will be available to express plurality.

Below, cursory definitions are provided with examples, mostly in English, and occasional and very brief mention of morpheme categories in other languages.

## Verbs
Most saliently, verbs include action words such as *run*, *walk*, *talk* and *throw*. But verbs also denote psychological events that don't entail much if any obvious physical activity: *think*, *see*, *hear* and *consider*. In most sentences, verbs are the core that other words and phrases in the sentence relate to. In *Zander ate the pasta*, the verb *ate* denotes an eating event in the past; an eater, *Zander*; and the stuff getting eaten, *the pasta*. There are technical issues involved in defining verbs in a consistent way across all languages, but it's likely that all languages have verbs or words that are very verb-like.

## Nouns
You might have learned that a noun is a word that names a person, place or thing. That definition has problems, but it's good enough on an intuitive level. Some nouns identify particular individuals and are called proper nouns, or names, such as *Thelma*, *Zack*, *the United Nations*. Nouns used less specifically, without reference to a particular individual, are common nouns: *cat*, *chair*, *laptop* as well as more abstract ones such as *thought*, *happiness* and *peculiarity*. Note that *talk* and *walk* are nouns as well as verbs, depending on how they're used in a sentence – a verb in *Erica talks a lot* but a noun in *Erica gave an interesting talk*. Like verbs, nouns or something very close to them are likely available in all languages.

## Adjectives
These typically modify nouns by ascribing some property to them. English adjectives usually precede the nouns they modify, as in *red*

*flower*, <u>*cold*</u> *beer*, <u>*scary*</u> *movie*. As mentioned above, according to some linguists, adjectives are likely a third universal category available in all languages.

This explanation of adjectiveness isn't very satisfactory, and we'll take a short digression to state the problem and then offer a better, more technical way to describe adjectives. Part of the problem is that there's no explanation of what *modify* means. Intuitively, an adjective modifies a noun by providing additional properties about the noun. But articles such as *the*, numerals such as *three* and the plural marker *-s* can also be said to modify nouns, although they aren't considered adjectives. And don't verbs provide properties as well, as in *Emma runs three times a week*, in which *runs three times a week* indicates a property of Emma just as much as *tall* would?

Let's look at Baker's (2003) reasoning about what adjectives are. First, his book is about lexical categories, which are generally assumed to include at least nouns, verbs and adjectives. He considers prepositions to be primarily functional and limits his theory to three lexical categories. Verbs are argued to be words that take arguments, i.e., things that do, experience or are otherwise affected by the verb. Nouns are things that can refer to entities in the world AND serve as the core of arguments, i.e., things that do, experience or are otherwise affected by the verb. In the example just above, *ate* is a verb that wants arguments, while *Zander* and *(the) pasta* fulfill the roles of the arguments. Given that, Baker then says that adjectives are the third lexical category that are neither nouns nor verbs. That's a bit weak for a definition, but Baker further notes that adjectives are modifiers that occur in certain environments, while nouns and verbs don't. For example, only words like *smart* can occur in the modifying position *a ___ woman* in the examples in (4). One caution, if you think (4b) is okay, rather than ungrammatical as indicated by the asterisk, that's because you're interpreting *genius woman* as a compound, not as a modifier plus noun, which Baker intends. (Compounds are discussed in Section 5.4.)

| | | |
|---|---|---|
| (4a) | a smart woman | (adjective-noun grammatical) |
| (4b) | *a genius woman | (noun-noun ungrammatical) |
| (4c) | *a shine woman | (verb-noun ungrammatical) |

Baker's is not the only argument about the status of adjectives as a special kind of modifier, but his argument has been briefly presented here to add additional heft to the meaning of what a modifier is and how exactly adjectives modify nouns.

A tangential point worth mentioning here is that, as much as morphologists would like to categorize word types, it's not the case that the classes of verb, noun and adjective, not to mention other classes, are cleanly separated categories. For one, they don't behave exactly the same across languages. In Japanese and Lakota, what seem like adjectives can take verbal suffixes like tense and agreement markers. And even within a language, words sometimes have properties of more than one category. Consider example (5), in which *bombing* is both verb-y and noun-y.

(5)    The enemy's bombing the civilians was horrible.

By virtue of the article *the* and the possessive noun *enemy's*, *bombing* is noun-like. Yet *bombing* also has a doer of the bombing, *the enemy('s)* and something affected by the bombing, *the civilians;* thus, *bombing*, in effect, has arguments, making it verb-like as well as noun-like.

**Adverbs**
Adverbs are also modifiers, but they are most often used with verbs: walk *fast*, read *carefully*, behave *oddly*. They can also modify adjectives, as in *curiously* refreshing. Adverbs seem to be a distinct class in many languages, though the form of adverb is often the same as the adjective. An example of this in English is *fast*, an adverb in walk *fast* and an adjective in *fast* runner.

**Prepositions**
Perhaps the main use of prepositions is to introduce phrases for indicating time, place, direction, manner and other functions: *in the house*, *on* time, *for* them. Some languages place the preposition after the noun phrase, in which case, they're called **postpositions**. The general category including prepositions and postpositions is **adpositions**. Likely, all languages have adpositions, though there seems to be much variation in the number of prepositions that languages have. Depending

on the definition, some languages have very few of them. English is particularly rich in prepositions, having dozens of them. English loves them so much it has developed a few by compounding simple prepositions into compounds such as *into* and *without*.

## Pronouns

These are forms that most often stand in for nouns or noun phrases. English personal pronouns include *they*, *she*, *he* and *it*. Possessive pronouns include *my*, *your* and *their*. Pronouns are another class likely appearing in all languages.

## Demonstratives

Demonstrative words have a basic function of pointing to things, physically or abstractly, with regard to spatial relationships, especially vis-à-vis the speaker and hearer. The demonstratives *this/these* suggest a relatively close relationship to the speaker, while *that/those* are used to indicate something relatively farther from the speaker. Some languages make more distinctions than just close to or far from the speaker. Demonstratives are probably present in nearly all languages, possibly all languages, as claimed by Diessel (1999, 1).

## Articles

A basic function of articles is to show specificity or definiteness, or the absence of specificity or definiteness, of something referred to. The English definite article is *the*; when a speaker refers to *the cat*, they assume the person they're talking with knows which cat is being referred to. The indefinite article is *a*. Many languages have only one article, and a good number of languages lack articles altogether. According to the World Atlas of Language Structures (wals.info), in a sample of 620 languages, about half the languages have either a dedicated word or affix corresponding to the English word *the* to indicate definiteness; indefinite markers are less frequent, and about a third of languages have neither a definite nor indefinite article (Dryer 2013e,f).

## Tense

Tense morphemes are used to refer to time of events or states expressed in a sentence. Usual tenses include past, present and future, though many languages lack distinct morphemes for making such a three-way distinction. On the other hand, some languages make finer distinctions, such as whether an event took place in the recent past or the distant past. In a WALS sample of 222 languages, 42% make a distinction between present and past tense, while nearly as many make no such present/past distinction (Östen and Velupillai 2013a). In such languages, the tense meaning is primarily inferred contextually or through the use of time words such as *now, yesterday, this morning* and *tomorrow*.

## Aspect

Related to tense, aspect markers suggest or entail whether an event is durational or instantaneous, completed or not. The *-ing* form of an English verb suggests ongoing activity, as in *We were swimming*. In contrast, the simple past, *We swam* deemphasizes the ongoingness and treats the swimming event as over and done with. One WALS sample counted languages that do or don't make some kind of morphological distinction between completed actions and incompleted actions, finding a slight preference for making such a distinction (Östen and Velupillai 2013b).

## Number

Singular and plural marking (e.g., *cat/cats*) is common among the world's languages, though by no means is the singular/plural distinction universal. English plural is more or less required for plural reference: *three cats/\*three cat*. Some languages have plural marking but only for restricted contexts. For example, plural might be used only with human nouns. A small minority of languages have dual number, a special marker for exactly two things as opposed to a more general plural for any amount more than one. According to WALS, more than 90% of a sample of 1,066 languages have some standard sort of way to mark plural (Dryer 2013d).

## Case

Case on nouns and other words usually marks the relationship of the noun phrase to the verb, for example, whether it's the subject or object of the verb. English has case forms only in its pronouns: the feminine pronoun in English may be *she* for subjects or *her* for objects, as in *She saw a fox* or *A fox saw her*. Many languages have much more extensive case systems, marking up to ten or more distinctions, usually with affixes on the noun. More than 60% of languages have some sort of case marking (Iggesen 2013).

**Affixes**
A general category of bound morphemes that appear on words for some of the functions we've mentioned so far, such as case, number, tense, etc. See the glossary entries for prefix, suffix, infix and circumfix.

**Complementizers**
These are grammatical indicators of a sentence within a sentence. In the complex sentence *The ancient Greeks knew that the earth is a sphere*, *that* introduces the subordinate clause *the earth is a sphere*, which itself is a sentence.

**Classifiers**
Morphemes that identify words as belonging to one of the various groups or classes are called classifiers, and they come in several kinds. Noun classifiers may identify a noun as animate, human, small, long, round, etc. Numeral classifiers may identify a noun class as well, but their main purpose is in counting. In Mandarin, *ge* is a numeral classifier used for both one and more than one: *yi ge xuesheng* ('one GE student'), *liang ge xuesheng* ('two GE student'). Closer to home, the Indo-European language Persian has at least one numeral classifier, *ta*, as in *se ta sib* ('three TA apple'). Numeral classifiers are fairly common, with perhaps a third of the world's languages having them (Gil 2013); English doesn't have numeral classifiers.

**Color Words**
Color words don't make up a major category like noun or verb, but they are a subset of adjectives. We discuss them separately here because much research over the past decades has found some interesting universal tendencies that involve not only language but also culture, anthropology and psycholinguistics. Besides, color words and the observation and analysis of the range of color words across languages is interesting and accessible to nonspecialists.

As far as we can tell, all languages have color words. As mentioned above, other potentially universal words include nouns, verbs, pronouns and demonstratives. A functional approach would suggest that all languages have a type of word because that type of word is extremely relevant for speakers to talk about the world. For example, it's extremely common to have a word for 'I' and 'we', as English has, but less common to have a form for 'me' and 'you' but not 'them'. Presumably, it's of practical importance to have words to indicate who's talking to who. Another area of intensive research is kinship terms, words for different family relationships. Some core kinship terms, such as words for 'mother', 'father', 'sister' and brother' are extremely common, as you might intuitively expect. But some languages have rich inventories of various familial relations that aren't present in other languages. The English word *aunt* is ambiguous with regard to, for example, whether the aunt is on the mother's side or the father's side; in contrast, Persian *xale* refers specifically to the mother's sister while *amme* is the word for the father's sister.

Here, we'll explore the class of color words. Apparently all languages have words for different colors, but languages vary in which and how many color words they have. What we'll focus on are so-called basic color terms – terms that seem to be essential to the language. Any language is able to express a wide variety of colors, their hues and shades and intensities, but some of those words are 'basic' while others aren't. For example, intuitively, we can rank *red* and *blue* as basic English color terms while ruling out *fuchsia* and *teal* as nonbasic.

There are various criteria to distinguish basic color terms from non-basic color terms. For one, basic terms are monomorphemic: *blue* is monomorphemic and potentially basic, while *sea foam* is multimorphemic and, thus, not basic. Another criterion is whether the term denotes a kind-of color. *Red* is just red, it's not a kind of some other color, and, therefore, it's potentially basic, but *vermilion* is a kind of red and, therefore, not basic. Importantly, if a color term is basic, all speakers know it. Any speaker of English knows the terms *red* and *blue*, though a good number of speakers are unclear, at best, on the meanings of *fuchsia* and *teal*. One final characteristic of basic terms that we'll mention is that a basic term doesn't rely on some indirect relationship to things in the world with that color. *Green* is just green and, therefore, potentially basic, while *fire-engine red* makes reference to fire engines, besides being multimorphemic. There are several other criteria for distinguishing basic from nonbasic color terms, but the ones just mentioned should suffice to illustrate that there's a principled and nonarbitrary way to determine which color terms are basic and which aren't.

It has been proposed that basic color terms across languages include the equivalent of the English words *white, black, red, yellow, green, blue, brown, purple, pink, orange, gray*. But not all languages have all these color terms. That, perhaps, is not surprising, but what is more interesting is that languages don't randomly choose some subset of the basic terms. They start with very basic color terms and add others in a systematic way.

Going back to Berlin and Kay (1969) and much subsequent research, by studying basic color terms in samples of languages, linguists have discovered that languages will nearly always have the equivalent of *black* and *white*; even if a language has no other basic terms, it will have at least these two terms. In such languages, *black* encompasses not only the color black but also darker colors of the spectrum, and the equivalent of *white* covers the lighter colors. If a language has other basic terms, they will follow in a certain implicational order. A language with only three basic terms will have *black* and *white* and add the equivalent of *red*. So, a three-term language won't have *blue, brown* and *purple*, for example, but only *black, white* and *red*. The rest of the basic terms will follow in a rather rigid order. A slightly larger inventory will include *green* and/or *yellow*, then *blue, brown* and, finally, in various orders, *purple, pink, orange* and *gray*. The presence of which basic terms are in a language is not arbitrary. Some sort of universal principle is operative.

## 3.6 Summary

This chapter provided a working definition of what words are along with preliminary answers to questions about the size of a speaker's vocabulary and the number of words that exist in a language. The chapter also briefly addressed how speakers gain a lexicon, through childhood acquisition and continued addition of words through life.

Then, a digression into historical and comparative linguistics showed that words, morphemes more generally, are passed down through the generations and that linguists can trace back from words in modern languages to reconstruct what those words' ancestors may have been like in sound and meaning thousands of years ago. Finally, we mentioned what kinds of morphemes appear in some languages' lexicons and how common or rare some kinds of morphemes are in languages.

## 3.7 Exercises

1. Estimate the size of your own vocabulary with the method presented in Section 3.3.
2. Any language's lexicon reflects certain aspects of the culture of the people that speak the language. If English has the word *laptop*, then we can guess that speakers of English have laptops, that they used to have laptops or, at least, that they're aware of laptops. Similarly, a reconstructed lexicon of a protolanguage may reveal something about the culture of the people who spoke it. Let's explore whether the lexicon of reconstructed Proto-Indo-European can reveal anything special about the culture of the people who spoke that language.

The reconstructed Proto-Indo-European words for 'mother', 'father', 'daughter', 'son', 'cloud' and 'water', among many others, aren't very informative, as we'd expect people of any culture to have words for such presumably basic and universally recognized things. But other words just might say something more culturally specific. For example, protowords for certain animals, plants and climate conditions may suggest the geographic location of a people.

Go to https://indo-european.info/dictionary-translator and scroll down to "Translate English to Indo-European", where you can request the Proto-Indo-European translation of English words.

Do a quick test by typing the English word *mother*, and you'll get two words, one close to *mater, the form we arrived at in our very simplified reconstruction based on words for 'mother' from only a few languages.

Then, search the Proto-Indo-European words for *alligator, banana, chimpanzee, coconut, palm* and *pineapple*. Second, search the

Proto-Indo-European words for *axle, bear, beech, birch, snow, wheel*. What are your results? What can you, tentatively, surmise about the speakers of Proto-Indo-European?

## 3.8 Arguable Answers to Exercises

1. You're likely to get a number in the tens of thousands.
2. You should come up with zilch for *alligator, banana, chimpanzee, coconut* and *pineapple* because there are no reconstructed roots for these words. They all refer to things associated with much warmer climates than near the Caspian Sea and were introduced to Indo-European languages through language contact with languages of more southern cultures. The one exception is *palm*, which does have a Proto-Indo-European root. Interestingly, it's the same root for *palm* of the hand. Possibly when speakers of Proto-Indo-European or its descendants became familiar with palm trees, they used the word for 'palm of the hand' metaphorically to refer to the palm leaves.

On the other hand, the *Indo-European Dictionary-Translator* returns the reconstructed roots for *axle, bear, beech, birch, snow* and *wheel*, meaning that Proto-Indo-European speakers of 6,000-some years ago were familiar with these items as part of their culture. The animal, tree and precipitation words suggest a more northern climate, while the existence of words for *axle* and *wheel* suggest something about their level of technology.

If you're interested in historical linguistics, there are many excellent introductory sources. Of general interest is Crowley and Bowern's very accessible *An Introduction to Historical Linguistics*. Mallory's *In Search of the Indo-Europeans: Language, Archaeology and Myth* provides more information and conjectures about the Proto-Indo-Europeans than you'd ever want to know but is a fascinating inquiry into methods for investigating just who the Proto-Indo-Europeans were. Finally, the *American Heritage Dictionary* (1992) has an excellent appendix about the Proto-Indo-European language along with a list of reconstructed roots and some of the words in modern languages that the roots have survived in.

# Chapter 4

# Inflectional Morphology

## 4.1 Preliminaries

If you've studied a foreign language in school, chances are you've come across tables like the following, containing six forms of the verb *cantāre* ('to sing') in Latin. The macron over some of the vowels means that those vowels are pronounced longer than the other vowels, but that's a phonetic distinction that's irrelevant here.

(1)  Present tense of *cantāre*

| Singular | | | Plural | |
|---|---|---|---|---|
| <u>1</u> | cantō | 'I sing' | cantāmus | 'we sing' |
| <u>2</u> | cantās | 'you.Sg sing' | cantātis | 'you.PL sing' |
| <u>3</u> | cantat | 'she, he, it sings' | cantant | 'they sing' |

Such tables are **paradigms**, arrangements of the different forms of a word along with their meanings and functions. For verbs, paradigms are typically organized by person (first, second, third) and number (singular and plural). The first-person singular form *cantō* means 'I sing', *cantāmus* means 'we sing', etc. The six forms in (1) are actually only a small part of the full paradigm for the Latin verb 'sing'. The full paradigm of Latin verbs involves not only some 90 one-word forms like those in (1) but also a few **imperatives**, **infinitives**, plus complex two-word forms of **auxiliary** and verb, and a large number of **participle** and **gerund** forms. Participles are verb forms that are accompanied by a helping verb such as *be* or *have*, as in *I have <u>left</u>* and *I am <u>leaving</u>*. A gerund is a verb behaving like a noun, as in <u>*Eating*</u> *pizza for*

DOI: 10.4324/9781003030188-4

*breakfast is enjoyable.* You can see some sample verb paradigms at https://en.wikipedia.org/wiki/Latin_conjugation. All these distinctions need not delay us here, but it's important to point out that Latin verb paradigms are quite complex compared to paradigms in English.

**Inflectional morphology** is the grammar of generating the various forms of words with their meanings and particular grammatical functions from **roots** (Stump 1998, 13–14). For the verb *cantō* above, the root is √CANT. To begin wordformation, the root becomes the verbal stem *cant-*, which then combines with the inflectional suffix *-ō* for the first-person singular present, the result being the wordform *cantō*, meaning 'I sing'. We can analyze the first-person plural inflection as *-āmus* to get the wordform for 'we sing'.

The number of inflected forms of a word can be as small as a single form or vast, with thousands of possible forms, depending on the language and the part of speech. This chapter takes a look at inflectional morphology across languages.

## 4.2 Formation of Wordforms

The richness of a paradigm depends on the inflectional resources of the language. Some languages, such as Latin, Crow and Cree, have lots of inflectional morphology, while languages such as Vietnamese have very little if any inflectional morphology. In terms of inflectional morphology, English sits toward the lower end of the scale, with a middling number of inflections for verbs and nouns and adjectives.

Similar to a paradigm is the concept of a **lexeme**, the collection of the inflected forms of a word and their meanings. Each particular form in a lexeme is a **wordform**, a single word comprising the simple stem and inflection(s): *sing, sang, sung* are three of the wordforms for the verb *sing*. As a convenience, we'll use the root sign and capital letters to designate both a root and a lexeme. Thus, we say that *sing, sang, sung* are three of the wordforms of √SING.

Each of the six slots in (1) is a wordform corresponding to some **grammatical word** that fulfills a certain grammatical function but maintains the basic meaning of the root: both *sing* and *sang* have to do with singing events, but *sing* is the grammatical word for the present while *sang* is the grammatical word for the past.

The relationship between wordforms and grammatical words is not one-to-one, as a single wordform may correspond to several grammatical words. For example, the wordform *walked* is both the past tense, as in *Emma walked through the park*, and the perfect participle, as in *Emma has walked through the park many times*.

Lexemes and paradigms are similar in being sets of wordforms associated with meanings and functions. The term lexeme, however, tends to carry a more theoretical status with it. More importantly, lexemes contain only single-word forms while paradigms also include multiple-word forms. For example, *sing*, *sang*, *sung* are members of both the lexeme and the paradigm for √SING, but the paradigm will also include the two-word construction *has sung* while the lexeme does not.

Languages vary in how rich their lexemes are in terms of the number of words, depending on the number of inflections available in the language. English lexemes are relatively small, and the inflected words in the lexeme remain relatively short. Other languages have large lexemes with many wordforms and may allow for multiple inflections that allow for rather long words.

## 4.3  Noun Inflections

### 4.3.1  Number

Noun lexemes in English are simple with few wordforms. One can make the argument that English nouns have only two wordforms corresponding to two grammatical words, shown in (2).

(2)  Lexeme for QUEEN (Version 1)
  <u>Singular</u>      <u>Plural</u>
  queen        queens

The two forms are for the category of **number**. In linguistics jargon, number doesn't refer to 1, 2, 3, etc., which are numerals, but to the distinction between one and more than one (putting aside negative numerals). In English, the wordform *queen* is the grammatical word for the singular, and *queens* is the plural grammatical word. One might ask, don't nouns also have possessive forms? Certainly, *queen's* looks like a word, and it has the corresponding grammatical meaning of possession. There's also the plural possessive, with a distinct ortho-graphic form regarding the placement of the apostrophe.

(3)  Lexeme for √QUEEN (Version 2)

| Singular | Plural | Singular Possessive | Plural Possessive |
|---|---|---|---|
| queen | queens | queen's | queens' |

However, putting aside orthographic conventions, as there aren't any apostrophes in spoken language, notice that the plural, singular posses-sive and plural possessive are phonetically identical, /kwinz/; that is, they have the same wordform. Therefore, a more linguistically precise expression of the lexeme might be as in (4).

(4)  Lexeme for √QUEEN (Version 3)

| Singular | Plural | Singular Possessive | Plural Possessive |
|---|---|---|---|
| queen | queens | queens | queens |

Thus, √QUEEN has two wordforms, with and without the -s, and four grammatical words, three of which are phonetically identical. Hence, we have a case of **homophony**, the same sound representing different meanings. In (4), the wordform with the suffix -s is ambiguous three ways.

However, let's revise Version 3 based on a technicality. While the possessive looks like an inflection in *queen's*, the possessive -s, it turns out, attaches to a phrase, not a single word. A **phrase** is a group of words that behave together as a unit. Consider the following expres-sions, in which the possessive -s is not always contiguous with the noun doing the possessing.

(5a)  the [queen]'s daughter
(5b)  the [queen of Wazmania]'s daughter
(5c)  the [queen who they interviewed]'s daughter
(5d)  the [queen that they talked to]'s daughter

In the first example, it appears that -s attaches to the noun *queen*, but the other three examples clearly show that the possession suffix is attaching variously to a noun other than *queen* itself, to a verb and to a preposition. A more comprehensive description of what's going on is that the -*s* isn't suffixing to a single word but is attaching in each case to a noun phrase, a group of words including the core noun and modifying material. In (5b) it's not Wazmania's daughter being referred to but the daughter of the entity indicated by the bracketed phrase *queen of Wazmania*. Similarly, in (5c) and (5d), the daughter belongs to the *queen who they interviewed* and the *queen that they talked to*. The general conclusion is that possessive -*s* attaches to a phrase, not just a noun. It so happens that in (5a), the noun phrase is a single unmodified noun. Therefore, it can be argued that the possessive form is not part of the noun lexeme, at least not in English. Thus, we revert to the original hypothesis for the lexeme √QUEEN.

(6) Lexeme for √QUEEN (Version 4 = Version 1)

| Singular | Plural |
|----------|--------|
| queen | queens |

Recalling morphophonology from Chapter 1, another technical point to keep in mind, not reflected in the -*s* spelling, is that -*s* has allomorphs, that is, various pronunciations. The plural is pronounced [z] in *queens*, but [s] in *cats* and [əz] in *churches*. So, the -*s* in Version 4 should be understood as a convenient abstract representation. Depending on the phonological analysis, we could choose one of the pronunciations as 'basic'. If /z/ is the basic, underlying, stored representation of the plural form, the phonology decides whether to pronounce it [z], [s] or [əz]. The allomorph is decided by the last sound in the root form: [z] after voiced sounds, [s] after most voiceless sounds, and [əz] after so-called sibilant sounds like [s, z, ʃ, ʒ, ʧ,ʤ]. Voiced sounds, produced with vibration of the vocal cords, include vowels, /b, d, g, v, z, n/, among others; voiceless sounds, lacking vocal cord vibration, comprise /p, t, k, f, s/ and others. Another phonological analysis leaves the plural even more abstract, simply as PL. In either case, to be more precise the lexeme should be listed, as in (7).

(7) Lexeme for √QUEEN (version 5)

| Singular | Plural |
|----------|--------|
| queen | queen/z/ or queen/PL/ |

Plural formation for words like *queen* involves **concatenation**, a linear sequencing of stem and inflection. This is the case for most nouns in English. However, there is another option for some irregular nouns that don't follow the pattern of *queen/queens*, as in the following pairs.

(8)  goose/geese, mouse/mice, man/men, foot/feet, tooth/teeth, woman/women

In all of the examples in (8), instead of the plural suffix, there is alternation of the vowels in the stem. These are examples of **ablaut**, inflection by changing a vowel of the stem.

Another irregular plural is *children*, which involves both a vowel change in the root and the addition of an old plural form, similar to the *oxen* plural of *ox* but with a mysterious *r* thrown in. Some other irregular plurals include the unexpected *knives* instead of *\*knifes*, the uninflected plural in *sheep/sheep*, *deer/deer*, and a good number of plurals based on borrowings from classical languages, such as *phenomenon/phenomena* and *stimulus/stimuli*. When two wordforms don't have any obvious phonetic relationship and, apparently, involve two separate stems, we have **suppletion**. The suppletive plural is rare in English, but it does occur in the relatively frequent word *people*, the usual plural of *person*.

Ablaut and suppletion are irregular morphological relationships in English because both the forms themselves and the words they operate on are unpredictable; they're also infrequent. Further, ablaut and suppletion aren't generalized to new nouns that enter the language, meaning that they're unproductive. In contrast, the *-s* plural applies to most nouns in English and is productive in that it's also used for new nouns that are added to the language. For example, the word *blog*, which seems to have entered English in the 1990s, has the regular plural form *blogs*.

Summing up, English noun lexemes are very simple: two grammatical words and, usually, two wordforms – one with and one without a plural inflection. Note that it has gone without mention that the English singular noun forms don't have an inflection; the uninflected form without a plural marker is interpreted as singular. Other languages, such as Italian in (9), may have dedicated inflections for both singular and plural.

(9)  ragazz-a/ragazz-e
     girl-Sg/girl-PL
     'girl/girls'

The examples in (9) also show that, in contrast to English, some Italian nouns require an inflection. The root itself $\sqrt{\text{RAGAZZ}}$, as a stem, doesn't stand as a word by itself.

A small number of languages mark number other than singular and plural. Lavukaleve, spoken on the Solomon Islands, has no morpheme for the singular, but it has two overt markers for plural: the **dual** suffix *-ul* for a plurality of exactly two, and *-vil* for 'more than two'. Data are from Terrill (1999, 96), cited in Vellupilai (2012, 160).

(10)  mulukita      mulukita-ul    mulukita-vil
      orange        orange-Dual    orange-PL
      'orange.Sg'   'two oranges'  'more than two oranges'

Dual marking is uncommon crosslinguistically, but there are even rarer number markers in some languages. As we saw in Chapter 3, Lihir, spoken in Papua New Guinea, makes five number distinctions in its pronouns through what looks like a combination of inflected and suppletive forms: singular, dual, **trial** for 'three', **paucal** for 'a few, but more than three', and plural for 'more than a few'. Data from Corbett (2000, 25).

(11)  Second-Person Pronoun 'you' in Lihir
      Singular   wa      'you.Sg'
      Dual       gol     'you two'
      Trial      gotol   'you three'
      Paucal     gohet   'you few'
      Plural     go      'you more than a few'

How many is few? And what's the boundary between 'you few' and 'you more than a few'? You'd need to do some extra fieldwork with Lihir speakers to determine how many second persons are required to pass the boundary between paucal and plural.

### 4.3.2 Gender

Not all Italian nouns are like *ragazz-a/ragazz-e* ('girl/girls'). For example, there's the *-o/-i* contrast.

(12)   ragazz-o/ragazz-i
       boy-Sg/boy-PL
       'boy/boys'

What's similar between the two singular/plural pairs is that both involve vowel alternations in the suffix to distinguish the singular and plural forms. The difference between the pairs is in which vowels are involved. In this case, the vowels are connected to grammatical gender of the nouns. **Gender** is a classification of nouns based on certain differences in behavior. A lot of Italian nouns involve the *-a/-e* alternation, while many others show the *-o/-i* alternation in the number suffixes. Nouns with the *-a/-e* alternation are so-called feminine nouns, while those with an *-o/-i* alternation are masculine. The terms *masculine* and *feminine* are conventional labels based on a few salient members of each class that correspond to biological sex, but gender itself is a purely grammatical category in Italian. The noun *banca* ('bank') is just as grammatically feminine as *ragazza* ('girl') despite the lack of any particular femininity in banks. Italian has two genders, German has three. Swahili has twentyish, depending on the variety of the language being spoken.

Because Italian number suffixes also say something about gender of the noun, the morphemes have more features than the regular English plural marker. Instead of just saying that *-e* and *-i* are plural morphemes, we should more precisely specify the gender features as well.

(13)   -a          -e          -o          -i
       -Sg.Fem     -PL.Fem     -Sg.Masc    -PL.Masc

### 4.3.3 Definiteness/Indefiniteness

The morphosyntax and semantics of definiteness and indefiniteness and how they are expressed morphosyntactically are very complex. Some analyses focus instead on the related and equally complex concept of specificity (Lyons 1999). For our purposes, the distinction between a definite reference and an indefinite reference can be characterized by two factors: which thing is being talked about, and who is assumed to know which thing is being talked about. Consider the following.

(14)    I got an email this morning. The email was from a cousin of mine.

The speaker first mentions *an email*, presumably knowing which email was received but also assuming that the hearer, the person they're speaking to, is being introduced to said email for the first time. Therefore, the indefinite article is used. Once the email has been mentioned and introduced into the conversation, the speaker can assume that the hearer has become aware of the email, so on this second mention, the speaker refers to *the email*, with the definite article. At the same time, in the second sentence, a previously unmentioned cousin is brought into the conversation, and on the cousin's first mention, the speaker refers to *a cousin*. The next mention would be a definite reference to *the cousin* or *this cousin* or *my cousin*; other definite references could be the cousin's name or a pronoun. An expression is definite if there is a particular referent and both the speaker and hearer know which referent that is. On the other hand, an expression is indefinite if the identity of the referent is unknown or unclear, at least to the hearer.

English uses the free morphemes *the* and *a*, the so-called definite and indefinite articles, (among other options) to make the definite/indefinite distinction. Some languages use morphology, attaching the equivalent of articles to the noun. Scandinavian languages typically have a form that serves as a marker of either indefinite or definite, depending on its position. In the Norwegian example below, when *en* precedes the noun as a free morpheme, the interpretation is indefinite; when it suffixes to the noun, the interpretation is definite. Data from Haugen (1990, 167–168).

(15)     en park          park-en
         a park           park-the
         'a park'         'the park'

Some languages, such as English, have both definite and indefinite morphemes, but, as we saw in Chapter 3, many languages lack one or the other, and it's not particularly rare for a language not to have any dedicated definite/indefinite morphemes. On the other hand, some languages make more nuanced distinctions with a range of morphemes. One example of a language with a host of inflections for definiteness and indefiniteness is Crow, which has five suffixes. The suffix -sh, pronounced [ʃ], corresponds closely to English *the*, as in (16a). The suffix -dak in (16d) is used when there might or might not be any deer to refer to. In (16e), the -t suffix is sometimes used in generic or habitual statements, in this case, referring to any winter. Finally, there are two indefinites, -m in (16d) for when the speaker has a specific referent in mind and the -eem suffix for a nonspecific indefinite, meaning that the speaker doesn't have a particular individual in mind, as in (16c). The suffixes are attached to different kinds of stems in Crow nouns, which we won't detail here, and the indefinite -m and -eem may end up being pronounced identically as [m]. The -k at the end of the sentence indicates that the sentence is declarative, a statement. Data adapted from Graczyk (2007, 226–233).

| (16a) | kalakón | john | úuxee-sh | oóxpi-k |
|---|---|---|---|---|
|  | then | john | deer-Def | shoot-Decl |
|  | 'John shot the deer'. | | | |
| (16b) | húuleesh | john | úuxa-m | íkaa-k |
|  | yesterday | john | deer-Indef | see-Decl |
|  | 'John saw a deer yesterday'. | | | |
| (16c) | bilée-(ee)m | húu-hkaa-h | | |
|  | water-Indef | come-Cause-Imper | | |
|  | 'Bring me some water'. | | | |
| (16d) | úux-dak | al-ákaa-wishi-ʔ | | |
|  | deer-Det | 2.A-see-exist-Q | | |
|  | 'Have you seen any deer?' | | | |
| (16e) | báalaa-t | sas-chihpashí-i-k | | |
|  | winter-Det | early-dark-hab-Decl | | |
|  | 'In winter, it gets dark early'. | | | |

In (16a), *úuxee-sh* means 'the deer', as in English, in which the speaker presumes the hearer knows which deer is being talked about. In (16b), *úuxa-m* means 'a deer', as in English, in which this is the first mention of the deer, in contrast to *bilée-(ee)m* in (16c), in which there is no specific water being referred to. The suffix in *úux-dak* in (16d) indicates that there may or may not be any particular deer to refer to, as it's a conditional statement. Finally, the -*t* suffix in *báalaa-t* (16e) refers to winters in general, not any specific winter or other.

### 4.3.4 Case

In morphology, **case** inflections show the nouns' and noun phrases' relationships to the rest of the sentence. Which case goes with which function varies across languages and even within a language. But simplifying, among the most common cases are nominative, which most often marks the subject of the sentence, and accusative, which indicates the direct object. The pronoun *she* is the nominative subject in (17a), while *her* is the accusative direct object in (17b).

(17a)   She saw Sami.
(17b)   Sami saw her.

Dative case typically marks the recipient or the indirect object of verbs. In the Turkish example in (18), the subject is not marked overtly for nominative, but the object, the thing being given, gets the accusative suffix -*yi*. while dative -*a* tells us that the child is the one receiving the apple. Data are from Kornfilt (1987, 636).

(18)   hasan   çocuğ-a   elma-yi   ver-di
       hasan   child-Dat   apple-Acc   give-Past
       'Hasan gave the apple to the child'.

Genitive case shows possession and similar relationships.

Some languages have extensive case marking on nouns. Polish has seven cases, which interact with number. As an illustration, the lexeme √PTAK ('bird') is shown in (19). Data are based on Stone (1990, 359).

| (19) | **Case and Number Inflection for √PTAK ('Bird') in Polish** | | |
|---|---|---|---|
| | Singular | Plural | Example Paraphrase in Context |
| nominative | ptak-∅ | ptak-i | 'The bird/birds (is/are flying)' |
| vocative | ptak-u | ptak-i | 'Oh, bird(s)!' |

| | | | |
|---|---|---|---|
| accusative | ptak-a | ptak-i | 'See the bird(s)' |
| genitive | ptak-a | ptak-ow | 'the bird's/birds' nest' |
| dative | ptak-owi | ptak-om | 'to the bird(s)' |
| instrumental | ptak-iem | ptak-ami | 'with/by the bird(s)' |
| locative | ptak-u | ptak-ach | 'on the bird(s)' |

In addition to some of the cases that were previously mentioned, Polish has vocative case for addressing someone or something, instrumental case showing when something is used as a tool or means to do something and locative case for where something is happening. The notation -∅ is meant to remind that there's no particular suffix for some grammatical word. Here, there's no specific suffix for the nominative singular, but the empty suffix position does contrast with the other forms with case that DO have an overt phonetic realization. The lexeme √PTAK, therefore, has seven cases and two numbers, yielding 14 grammatical words. However, because *ptaki*, *ptaka* and *ptaku* are each, at least, ambiguous in two ways, there are only 10 distinct wordforms. Again, each particular affixal morpheme has at least two relevant features. For example, the suffix *-a* is [Accusative, Singular] or [Genitive, Singular]. Even more extensive in its case system than Polish is Finnish, whose nouns with their inflections show 30 forms for 15 cases and the two numbers singular and plural (Branch 1990, 607).

### 4.3.5 Pronouns

As seen in Section 4.3.4, English shows a case distinction for pronouns, depending on their function in a sentence. The feminine pronoun is *she* for the subject of a verb but *her* for the direct object. There's no affixation involved; rather, English simply has distinct lexical items for gender, case and number. Some of the pronoun forms in Spanish are more compositional than in English with identifiable suffixes. A gender distinction is clear between feminine *él* ('he, it') and *ella* ('she, it'). Also, an additional affix is added for plurality: *ellos* ('they' – Masculine) and *ellas* 'they' – Feminine). Note that the masculine and feminine plurals have a final *-s* in common while differing in the preceding vowel.

The variety of Loma spoken in Liberia has pronouns that are interesting because they have unexpected verbal information in the morphology as well as more typical nominal information such as number. The pronouns also show both concatenative morphology in the segments of consonants and vowels as well as nonconcatenative morphology with tones. In the paradigm below, the top column identifies the person and number of the pronoun. 'Incl' means inclusive, plural 'we', including the speaker and the hearer, i.e., 'me and you'; 'Excl' means exclusive, plural 'we' excluding the hearer, i.e., 'me and them but not you'. The diacritics refer to tones, pitches on the vowels that can distinguish words: ´ for high tone and ` for low tone. Data from Gleason (1961, 122–23).

(20)   Loma Pronoun Forms

|          | 1.Sg | 1PL. Incl | 1.PL. Excl |
|----------|------|-----------|------------|
| Present  | gè   | dé        | gé         |
| Future   | gà   | dá        | gá         |
| Negative | gɛ̀  | dɛ́       | gɛ́        |
| Habitual | gɔ̀  | dɔ́       | gɔ́        |

Let's look at a few of the forms to point out exactly what they mean. The form *gè* means 'I' when used for the present-tense meaning of a verb. For the future, the form *gà* 'I (will)' is used. Among the inclusive forms, *dé* means 'you and me, not them'. A number of regular correspondences show up. The *d-* appears only in the inclusive forms, leaving *g-* in the other forms. The high tone ´ pops up in the plural forms but not in the singular. And each of the vowels lines up with either present, future, negative or habitual.

### 4.3.6 Portmanteau Inflections

Above, it was noted that Italian noun inflections have two features: gender and number. For example, *-i* is [Masculine, Plural]. It's quite common for languages to have complex inflections like this, in which a single morpheme indicates more than a single meaning and/or function. A morpheme that bundles two or more meanings and functions is called a **portmanteau** morpheme. A few more examples show various cases of bundling more than a single feature into morphemes.

Persian has two morphemes that conjoin definiteness with number and case. The first involves number and definiteness. The meaning contrast in the translations of the sentences in (21a and b) shows that *-ha* is not only plural but also definite and/or specific. The # signals that the sentence can't have the meaning suggested in the particular translation, here the nonspecific meaning.

(21a)   gorbeh-ha        birun        mixabænd
        cat-PL           outside      are.sleeping
        'The cats are sleeping outside'
        #'(Some) cats are sleeping outside'

In (21a), the only interpretation is that some particular cats, say our cats, are outside sleeping, not that there are some arbitrary cats out there sleeping. So, the gloss for *-ha* is more precisely as in (21b), in which the gloss shows the morpheme has the features [Plural, Definite].

(21b)   gorbeh-ha        birun        mixabænd
        cat-PL.Def       out          are.sleeping
        'The cats are sleeping outside'.

One caution, though not crucial to the main point here about portmanteau morphemes, is that saying *-ha* is plural is perhaps oversimplifying. For example, Windfuhr (1990, 533) claims that more generally *-ha* should be interpreted as having an "amplification" function, as it can also be used with mass nouns like *ab* 'water'; *ab-ha* can mean 'lots of water' as well as a plurality of individual water units. It's sometimes the case that a general notion like plural, and, therefore, a meaning gloss such as [PL] doesn't necessarily mean exactly the same thing across languages.

Also joining up with definiteness to form a portmanteau inflection in Persian is case. The suffix *-ra* (pronounced variously as [ra], [ro] and [o]) is most often used as a direct object or accusative marker, not used on subjects.

(22a)   gorbe        muʃ-o            did
        cat          mouse-Acc        saw
        'The cat saw the mouse'.

But also note the translation of the intended meaning of *muʃ-o*: *the mouse*, meaning that the cat saw a particular mouse, not some indefinite mouse.

Because *-ra* is a case marker only for objects that are definite, we can gloss (22a) more precisely as (22b), with the features [Acc; Definite].

| (22b) | gorbe | muʃ-o | did |
|---|---|---|---|
| | cat | mouse-Acc.Def | saw |
| | 'The cat saw the mouse'. | | |

Giving full disclosure at this point, it should be noted that the function of *-ra* is actually more complex than presented here, as it appears to have functions other than marking a definite object. Linguists are still trying to account for what *-ra* does in Persian in a theoretically satisfying way (e.g., Samavati 2022).

### 4.3.7 Nonconcatenative Inflection

With the exception of ablaut plurals such as *mouse/mice* and a few other forms, the inflectional morphology, so far has, been mostly concatenative. For example, the regular plural *-s* concatenates with *cat* in a linear sequence of morphemes to form the plural form *cats*. The Persian example just above concatenates the definite direct object suffix *-o* on the stem *muʃ* to get *muʃ-o*.

Some inflection, however, involves something other than a linear sequence of morphemes. English has some nonconcatenating morphology. The plural forms of some irregular nouns are nonconcatenating, as in the ablaut pair *man/men*. As another example, there are several dozen noun/verb pairs in English that are distinguished by different placement of the main stress over the same sequence of vowels and consonants. In these pairs of words, if the stress is on the first syllable, the word is a noun; stress on the second syllable results in a verb. Here, we use capital letters to mark the syllable with strong main stress. The pronunciation of the vowel may change because of the stress. The main thing to observe is that there's no morpheme that's attached to the left or right of the stem; rather, what that marks the difference between nouns and verbs in these pairs is the stress, which is, in a sense, on top of the consonants and vowels, not linearly adjacent to them.

(23)  | Noun | Verb |
      |------|------|
      | CONvert | conVERT |
      | PERvert | perVERT |
      | REcord | reCORD |
      | DEfect | deFECT |
      | CONtest | conTEST |
      | PREsent | preSENT |

Some languages can use tones for inflection. **Tones** are various pitches, independent of the segment or syllable they're associated with, that can distinguish words. In Hausa, spoken in western Africa, mostly in Nigeria and Niger, *góoràa* with a high tone on the first syllable and low tone on the second syllable means 'bamboo'; *gòoráa* with the opposite tone pattern means 'large gourd'. Both words have the same sequence of consonants and vowels, so it's the tone pattern that makes the lexical distinction. Tones can also be used inflectionally to make grammatical distinctions. Noni, spoken in Cameroon, has plurals formed by a change in tone. A low–high pattern is singular, while a high tone is plural. Data from Hyman (2000, 590), cited in Booij (2009, 4).

(24)  | LH pattern | H pattern | LH pattern | H pattern |
      |------------|-----------|------------|-----------|
      | bwě | bwé | jĭn | jín |
      | dog.Sg | dog.PL | maggot.Sg | maggot.PL |
      | 'dog' | 'dogs' | 'maggot' | 'maggots' |

A final noun-inflection example illustrates another nonlinear kind of morphology. Recall the Arabic noun examples from Chapter 2 (McCarthy 1979, 244; 1981, 374; cited in Lieber 2016; Fromkin et al. 1999, 42).

(25a)   kaatib      'writer'
(25b)   kitaab      'book'
(25c)   kutuub      'books'

What the three nouns have in common is the *k-t-b* sequence of consonants, a so-called triconsonantal root that's common in Semitic languages. What distinguishes the three words are the vowels and where they're placed. Because the vowels are interrupting the triconsonantal root, they look like a kind of infix. But unlike infixes, the inserted vowels are discontinuous. What seems to be going on is a two-tiered morphology rather than a simple linear concatenating morphology. To make the word for 'writer', we would insert *aa* between the first two consonants and an *i* between the last two. For singular 'book', we would insert the two vowels *i* and *aa* in those positions, and for plural 'books', we would insert a *u* and *uu*.

(26a)  'writer'  consonantal tier    k ___ t ___ b
                                          ⇑     ⇑
            inflectional tier             aa    i

(26b)  'book'   consonantal tier    k ___ t ___ b
                                          ⇑     ⇑
            inflectional tier             i     aa

(26c)  'books'  consonantal tier    k ___ t ___ b
                                          ⇑     ⇑
            inflectional tier             u     uu

The morphology in Arabic and other Semitic languages, such as Hebrew, is evidence that there are alternatives to strictly linear inflectional morphology. Indeed, we've already seen examples of suppletion, such as *sing/sang*, that don't adhere to the notion that inflectional morphology always builds words as a sequential string of morphemes. In the examples in (26), we can say that one morpheme is the *ktb* root, or $\sqrt{\text{KTB}}$. The other morphemes are the vowels that are inserted at various positions within the root.

The same kind of analysis is applicable for the Noni example above in (27), in which tones have inflectional value. In that case, the words involve a segmental tier for the vowels and consonants and a parallel tonal tier. The segmental tiers are identical for the singular and plural forms, while the tones are distinct.

| (27a) | | bwě 'dog. Sg' | (27b) | bwé |
|---|---|---|---|---|
| Tonal Tier | | LH | | H |
| Segmental Tier | | bwe | | bwe |
| | | LH pattern | | H pattern |
| | | bwě | | bwé |
| | | dog.Sg | | dog.PL |

For a detailed discussion of nonlinear morphology, see Spencer (1991, Chapter 5).

Another kind of nonlinear relationship among morphemes occurs when a feature of one morpheme correlates with another morpheme. There's still a sequence of morphemes, but the same information is reflected in both. Take the Latin verb *frangō* ('I break'). The -*ō* agreement suffix is the same as that in the word *cantō* ('I sing') in example (1), indicating a subject of first-person singular. That leaves *frang*- as the bound stem for the verb 'break'.

(28)    frang-ō
        break-1.Sg
        'I break'

The perfect of this verb is *frēgī* ('I have given' or 'I gave'). It looks like the stem in this case is *frēg*-.

(29)    frēg-ī
        break.Perf-1.Sg
        'I have broken'

The vowel differs between the two stems, but the consonants vary as well: the present has an *n* that doesn't show up in the perfect. While, traditionally, verbs like this in Latin are analyzed as organizing on two separate stems, they can also be analyzed in a nonsequential way with a stem of *frg* from the root √FRG and the rest of the words related overlappingly to the tense and aspect. R indicates the root common to both present and past.

(30a)   f    r    a       n      g    -ō
        R    R    Pres     Pres   R    -Pres.1.Sg
(30b)   f    r    ē              g    -ī
        R    R    Perfect         R    -Perfect.1.Sg

On this view, what we have then is a common stem, *frg*, and alternate vowels in the stem, *a* and *ē*, whose functions overlap with the suffixes, -*ō* and -*ī* . The point being that perhaps nonlinear morphology isn't as exotic as first appeared. Latin and English have some forms that can be analyzed similarly to words in Arabic.

## 4.4 Verb Inflections

Languages often show more inflectional variation in their verbs than in their nouns; that is, verb lexemes tend to be larger than noun lexemes in both the number of wordforms and the number of grammatical words. In English, however, verbs have a smaller amount of variation. Regular verbs, such as *cook* and *rub* below, have a single stem, which is used in a bare form or gets suffixed with the suffixes *-s*, *-ed* and *-ing*. Irregular verbs vary in the stem as well, as in *eat*, *go* and *cut*.

| (31) | bare | 3 Sg Present | Past | Present Participle | Perfect/Passive Participle |
|------|------|--------------|------|-------------------|----------------------------|
|      | cook | cooks | cooked | cooking | cooked |
|      | rub | rub | rubbed | rubbing | rubbed |
|      | eat | eats | ate | eating | eaten |
|      | go | goes | went | going | gone |
|      | cut | cuts | cut | cutting | cut |

The five grammatical words for the verbs are identified on the top row, but the list is somewhat simplified. The bare grammatical word has a number of functions. For example, it's used in the present tense for all persons and numbers except third-person singular, as in (32a); as part of the *to*-infinitive, as in (32b) and as the bare infinitive, as in (32c). The *-s* form fills in the gap for the third-person singular present (32d).

(32a)   Pat and Alex cook together on weekends.
(32b)   Pat and Alex like to cook together on weekends.
(32c)   Pat helps Alex cook on weekends.
(32d)   Pat cooks on weekends.

The *-ed* suffixed to the verb stem makes it past, but that form is used in several other ways as well, for example, a conditional or hypothetical.

(33a)   Alex cooked an inedible lasagna.
(33b)   If I cooked snails with butter, would you eat them?

The present participle form, in conjunction with the auxiliary *be*, is typically used for ongoing durational activity, as in (34a), but it can also be used as a noun, the so-called gerund, as in (34b), and adjectivally, as in (34c).

(34a)   The lasagna is cooking.
(34b)   Cooking is Alex's way of relaxing.
(34c)   Alex prefers a Mediterranean cooking style.

The fifth grammatical word could be split into two grammatical words, but they're always the same form in English. The perfect participle is used with the auxiliary *have*.

(35)   Pat and Alex have cooked a goose.

While the passive participle is the same form, it has a different meaning and function in forming the passive form of the verb with some form of the verb *be*.

(36)   The goose was cooked by Alex and Pat.

Among the sample verbs in (31) the regular verbs have four distinct wordforms for the five grammatical slots: *eat* and *go* have five distinct forms, one for each grammatical word, and *cut* has only three distinct forms. Despite the variation, the total number of verb forms in any particular lexeme is quite limited in English.

As previously mentioned, many languages have much larger lexemes than English. At the beginning of this chapter, we saw the paradigm for the present tense of Latin *cantāre* ('to sing'), comprising six wordforms over six grammatical slots based on person and number. But that was only for the present tense. A typical full verbal lexeme in Latin is in the range of a hundred wordforms, reflecting not only person and number but also tense, aspect and mood. Turkish verbal lexemes are much larger still. Gleason (1961, 112–116) illustrates 21 of the more important suffixes used for person and number of the subject, tense, whether the verb is seen as habitual and/or continuous, negative, and other functions. The 21 suffixes come in ten 'orders', referring to the sequential left-to-right order of the suffixes on the verb stem. Not all suffixes are present in any given wordform; in fact, some of the suffixes are mutually exclusive. Despite those constraints, there's still the possibility of long sequences of suffixes combining for a multitude of wordforms. One example is in (37), in which the stem for 'break' has five suffixes, based on Gleason (1961, 114). The /ɨ/ sound is similar to the schwa in English.

(37) kir-il-ma-di-lar-mi
    break-Pass-Neg-Past-3.PL.Subj-Q
    'Weren't they broken?'

Let's look carefully at what's going on. There's a stem verb meaning 'break' on the extreme left, followed by a strictly ordered series of suffixes. The leftmost suffix, -il, makes the verb passive, yielding the meaning 'be broken'. The next suffix, -ma, is a negative, resulting in 'not be broken'. Then -di puts the verb in the past, yielding 'weren't broken'. The suffix -lar is an agreement marker, indicating a third-person plural subject, showing up in the translation as 'they' – the cumulative result, at this point, being 'they weren't broken'. Finally, the rightmost suffix -mi converts the whole sequence to question, resulting in 'weren't they broken?'.

Here's an even more fun Turkish example, based on Lieber (2016, 136), citing Inkelas and Orgun (1998).

(38)
| çekoslovakya- | | | li- | laş- | tir- | ama- | yacak- |
|---|---|---|---|---|---|---|---|
| Czechoslovakia- | | | from- | become- | Cause- | unable- | Future- |
| lar- | imiz- | dan- | | mi- | ydi- | niz | |
| PL- | 1.PL- | Ablative- | | Q- | Past- | 2.PL | |

'Were you from those (who) we will be able to cause to become Czechoslovakians?'

Gleason (1961) claims that, even with various restrictions, whereby some suffixes are incompatible with others, a Turkish verb has more than 3,000 wordforms for the various grammatical words. We'll see in the next chapter, when derivational morphology is also part of the picture, that in some languages, the number of words you can make can reach into the millions. English verbs, with only five possible forms, are quite simple and, intuitively, something we can conceive of as a list of sorts that we access for the right form in a particular context. But a Turkish verb with 3,000+ wordforms is a horse of a different color. Do Turkish speakers really list all those forms in their lexicon? It's hard to think that's the case, for if Turks have, say, 5,000 verbs, that results in 15 million wordforms nestled in the lexicon. For one, perhaps many of the forms are unattested, in that no one has ever used them or, at least, any given Turkish speaker may not have used or heard them. Second, we noted that some of the forms are predictable and need not be listed.

For example, the English third-person singular present forms with -s are perfectly predictable and are better left to morphology than with lexical entries. (The exception is modal verbs like *should*, *might*, *can*, etc., which don't take present -s.) Similar for the -*ing* forms. Because the lexicon is the repository of arbitrary sound-meaning pairs, they need not be listed. As examples, consider the following example verbal lexemes, in which R indicates a predictable regular form that need not be listed in the lexicon.

(39)

| bare | 3 Sg Present | Past | Present Participle | Perfect/Passive Participle |
|------|--------------|------|--------------------|----------------------------|
|      | -s           | -ed  | -ing               | -ed                        |
| cook | R            | R    | R                  | R                          |
| rub  | R            | R    | R                  | R                          |
| eat  | R            | ate  | R                  | eaten                      |
| go   | R            | went | R                  | gone                       |
| cut  | R            | cut  | R                  | cut                        |

That is, strictly speaking, not all the wordforms are in the lexicon on the assumption that predictable forms aren't listed. Perhaps that principle reduces the memory load of Turkish speakers.

This ability to construct a verb with so many affixes is a property of an **agglutinating** structure, in which a string of affixes yield a long word. Each suffix tends to have a single dedicated contribution to the whole meaning: in (38), *tir-* for 'from', *laş-* for 'become', *yacak-* for future tense, *mi-* to make a question, *ydi-* for past tense and so on. This contrasts with morphology in **fusional** languages, in which affixes typically carry a number of functions. Latin and English are fusional languages. For example, the English verbal suffix -s comprises information for third-person singular subject, present tense, indicative mood, in bracketed feature notation -s = [3, Sg, Subj, Present, Indicative] – a lot of grammatical information packed into one little -s!

Languages with no or very little morphology are called **isolating** languages, in which each word tends to be a single morpheme.

### 4.4.1 Agreement

Another common kind of inflection is agreement. **Agreement** is a relationship between elements in a sentence such that features in one element call for corresponding features to be morphologically expressed in another element. Agreement is sometimes called concord, depending on the particular type of agreement. We've seen agreement in Latin, English and Turkish, whereby the person and number of the subject of a sentence requires an affix on the verb reflecting the same person and number. For example, in the sentence *Anna thinks quinoa is overrated*, the verb form *thinks*, with the *-s* suffix for third-person singular, agrees with the third person singular subject *Anna*. English has minimal subject-verb agreement, and some languages have none. But a good number of languages have much more agreement between a verb and its arguments, as we saw in Latin. To discuss agreement more fully, let's provide a notion of what an argument is.

An **argument** is a phrase required by some word. Focusing on verbs, each verb calls for one or more arguments of certain kinds. These arguments, which denote which things are taking part in the event specified by the verb, are, more or less, required in order for the sentence to be grammatical. The verb *sleep* is a one-argument verb, requiring and allowing only a subject. If we either remove the argument or add another one the result is ungrammatical.

(40a)   The cat is sleeping.
(40b)   *Is sleeping
(40c)   *The cat is sleeping the blanket

The verb *denounce* wants two arguments, a subject doing the denouncing and a direct object being denounced. If the subject argument or object argument is left off, the result is ungrammatical.

(41a)   The protestors denounced the tyrant.
(41b)   *Denounced the tyrant
(41c)   *The protestors denounced

Another kind of argument is the indirect object, the goal of the action, the thing to which the direct object is directed. In English the indirect object often comes with the preposition *to*. The verb *give* has three arguments, a subject, a direct object and an indirect object. Omitting any of the arguments leaves us with an ungrammatical result.

(42a)   Jennie gave the flu to her mom.
(42b)   *Jennie gave the flu
(42c)   *Gave the flu to her mom.
(42d)   *Jennie gave to her mom

Not all elements that accompany the verb are arguments. Optional, modifying material and certain other phrases are adjuncts. In *Jenna went home*, the word *home*, though it looks like it's in the direct object position, is not required by the verb. The verb *went* is intransitive and doesn't want a direct object. Further, remove *home* from the sentence, and the result is still a perfectly fine if somewhat bare English sentence: *Jenna went*.

Features of arguments that the verb agrees with commonly involve person and number. **Person** refers to whether the argument is first person, for example *I* or *we*; second person, e.g., *you*; third person, e.g., *she*, *he*. Recall that number refers to singular and plural. English has minimal agreement on verbs, but historical remnants of a richer agreement system still exist with the verb *to be*. In the present tense, the wordforms vary by person and number, though not all grammatical words are distinct.

(43)   **Agreement of *to be* with its subject**

| I am | we are |
|------|--------|
| you are | you are |
| she, he it is | they are |

Because the only argument present is the subject, it's clear that the English word *be* agrees with the person and number of the subject. Subject agreement on the verb is much more robust in other languages, for example, in Persian, in which it appears for all verbs in the present tense. The *mi-* prefix can, here, be interpreted as progressive, corresponding to the *-ing* form of verbs in English. The examples are from colloquial Persian. In the third-person plural, the final *d* is written in Persian but usually not pronounced.

(44)   Persian *xordæn* 'eat'

| mæn | mi-xor-æm | 'I am eating' |
| to | mi-xor-i | 'you.Sg are eating' |
| u | mi-xor-e | 'he/she is eating' |
| ma | mi-xor-im | 'we are eating' |
| shoma | mi-xor-in | 'you.Pl are eating' |
| unha | mi-xor-æn(d) | 'they are eating' |

Some languages' verbs inflect to show agreement with both the subject and the direct object, as in Kanuri, spoken in Nigeria and neighboring countries. Data are from Hutchison (1981, 135), cited in Croft (1990, 106). The diacritics indicate tones. The gloss Perf indicates perfective aspect, meaning an action has been completed.

(45)  nzú-rú-kə́-nà
      2.Sg.Obj-see-1.Sg.Subj-Perf
      'I saw you'.

The Kanuri verb is quite complex, with two agreement inflections: the prefix *nzú-* for the second-person singular direct object 'you' in the English translation and the suffix *-kə́* for the first-person singular subject 'I'. We'll return to multiple affixes later but note here that the perfective suffix is added to a stem that already has an agreement suffix. Also note in the Kanuri example that the object agreement affix *nzú-* precedes the verb, while the subject agreement *-kə́* follows the verb. Placement of agreement affixes varies across languages. One example from Choctaw, a Muskogean language of North America, shows both agreement morphemes as prefixes, *is-* for the subject corresponding to 'you' in English and *sa-* for the object, corresponding to 'me'. Data based on Baker (2003, 251, citing Davies 1986).

(46)  is-sa-hottopali-tok
      2.Sg.Subj-1.Sg.Obj-hurt-Past
      'You hurt me'.

Abaza, a language of the Caucasus region, shows agreement with four arguments in the following causative construction, along with a number of other affixes. The letter y is used instead of IPA j and sounds like English y in *yellow*. Data from Allen (1956, cited in Whaley 1997, 165) and Koshevoy (2018).

(47)  aləgaζʷ                  ácʸkʷəncʷakʷa    llá    aphʷə́pa
      boys                     old.man          dog    girl
      y-gʸ-y-z-d-m-l-r-ətxd
      3.Sg-Neg-3.Pl-Potential-3.Sg.Human-Neg-3.Sg.Fem-Cause-give
      'The old man couldn't make the boys give the girl her dog back'.

Don't worry about the sounds represented by the unfamiliar symbols but do look at that long string of prefixes made of a single sound each. Just to be clear, let's analyze the morphemes in the long verb construction. The verbal stem -*ətxd* ('give') is the rightmost element. To its immediate left is *r*-, glossed as Cause – together they mean 'cause to give' or 'make someone give'. Negation appears twice, as *g*ʸ- and *m*-, while *z*- is 'Potential', or 'can, could'. So far, we have 'could not make give'. That leaves the agreement markers *y*-, *y*-, *d*- and *l*-. The third morpheme in the verb is *y*-, glossed as 3.PL, which must, therefore, agree with *aláɡaζʷ* 'boys' because that's the only plural argument in the sentence. Of the three 3.Sg morphemes, the *l*- third from the right is glossed as Feminine so it must be agreeing with *aphʷə́pa* ('girl'), the indirect object of 'give'. That leaves two 3.Sg agreement morphemes, the initial *y*- and the *d*- appearing fifth from the left. In addition to being 3.Sg, the *d*- is also glossed as human, so it's the agreement marker for *ácʸkʷəncʷakʷa* ('old man'), the subject of the verb. The initial *y*- is left to agree with the only remaining argument, *llá* ('dog'). Below are the morphemes as they appear in linear order in the verb.

(48)   y      3.Sg, agrees with *llá* 'dog'
       gʸ     Negative, negates Potential *z*-, resulting in 'could not'
       y      3.Pl, agrees with *aláɡaζʷ* 'boys'
       z      Potential 'could'
       d      3.Sg.Human, agrees with *ácʸkʷəncʷakʷa* 'old.man'
       m      Negative, with *g*ʸ, like a circumfix, Neg affixation appears in two positions
       l      3.Sg.Fem, agrees with *aphʷə́pa* 'girl'
       r      Cause, equivalent to 'make' in the translation
       ətxd   'give'

English and Persian, among many languages, show verbal agreement with the subject; English minimally does this for third-person singular present. Kanuri, Choctaw and Abaza are examples of languages that show verbal agreement with more than one argument, with a separate agreement morpheme for each agreement with an argument. Some languages package the agreement information with multiple arguments in a single morpheme, as in Hixkaryana, a Carib language of Brazil. The gloss ImmPast for the suffix -*no* indicates that the event took place in the immediate, recent past. Data are from Derbyshire (1979, 148).

(49a)  ki-tayma-no
       1S/2O-push-ImmPast
       'I pushed you'.
(49b)  mi-ka-no
       2S/3O-say-ImmPast
       'You said it'.

The prefix *ki-* in (49a) tells us two things: that the subject is first person 'I' AND that the object is second person 'you'. In the other example, *mi-* reflects both second-person subject 'you' and third-person object 'it'.

Also note in the Choctaw, Kanuri and Abaza examples above that there are no expressed arguments independent of the verb for the agreement markers to agree with. Another language in which the verb behaves similarly is Crow. Data from Graczyk (2007, 122–123).

(50)   dii-waa-lit-úu
       2.B-1.A-hit-Pl
       'I hit you.Pl'/'we hit you.Sg'

The information about the first-person subject, glossed 1.A, and the second-person object, 2.B, is solely on the verb. Languages in which arguments need not appear outside the verb are sometimes called prodrop languages, but it might also be the case that the verbal affixes are actually the arguments. Graczyk (2007) argues that this is the case for Crow.

## Other Agreement

Languages can have agreement relations between other parts of the sentence besides verbs and their arguments. For example, in French, both articles and adjectives agree in number and gender with the nouns they modify. The noun *voiture* ('car') is grammatically feminine, and 'the green car' is *la voiture verte* [la vwatyr vɛrt], with the feminine article *la* and the feminine form of 'green' *verte*. In contrast, *le camion vert* ('the green truck') [lə kamjɔ̃ vɛr] has the masculine article and adjective, *le* and *vert*, agreeing with the masculine noun *camion*; note that the masculine form for 'green' doesn't pronounce the t that appears in the spelling. If the noun is plural, the article and adjective reflect plurality as well: *les voitures vertes* [le vwatyr vɛrt] ('the.PL cars green. Fem.PL') and *les camions verts* [lə kamjõ vɛr] ('the.PL truck green. Masc.PL'), although the final *-s* plurals aren't pronounced. The plural article is phonetically identical for both masculine and feminine adjectives.

### 4.4.2 A Few Other Verbal Affixes

A few other examples illustrate other verbal inflections that languages have. Japanese verbs, for example, can host a number of inflections. In (51a), the *-ru* suffix can be interpreted as a present tense marker. Change it to *-ta* for the past tense (51b). The morpheme *ga* means that the preceding expression, *hiro* is the subject, while *o* indicates the object. Japanese doesn't have definite and indefinite articles, so the word *pitsa* is ambiguous with regard to definiteness. It's also ambiguous for number; that is, the sentence doesn't tell us whether Hiro ate one or more pizzas. In Japanese, number and definiteness can usually be inferred from context.

| (51a) | hiro | ga | piza | o | tabe-ru |
|---|---|---|---|---|---|
| | hiro | Nom | pizza | Acc | eat-Pres |
| | 'Hiro is eating a/the pizza/s' | | | | |
| (51b) | hiro | ga | piza | o | tabe-ta |
| | hiro | Nom | pizza | Acc | eat-Past |
| | 'Hiro ate a/the pizza/s' | | | | |

Context is important as, unlike in some languages that we've seen so far, Japanese doesn't have any person marking on the verb.

To make a passive, the suffix *-rare* appears, preceding the tense suffix *-ta*.

| (52) | piza | ga | tabe-rare-ta |
|---|---|---|---|
| | pizza | Nom | eat-Pass-Past |
| | 'A/The pizza was eaten' | | |

The sentences above are understood as declarative or statements of fact. Just as in English, rising intonation can be used to make a question, so with the right intonation, these sentences can also be questions.

However, Japanese also has a dedicated suffix to indicate a question, -*ka*. The *mas*- makes the form more polite.

(53)  hiro  ga  piza  o  tabe-mas-u-ka
      hiro  Nom  pizza  Acc  eat-Polite-Pres-Q
      'Is Hiro eating a/the pizza?'

Question inflections are fairly common crosslinguistically. Another language with a question inflection is Crow. Ordinary statements end with -*k*, the declarative marker, as in (54a), which simply makes a statement. To make a question, the -*k* is replaced with the glottal stop -*ʔ*, as in (54b). Data adapted from Graczyk (652007, 227).

(54a)  húuleesh  john  úuxa-m  íkaa-k
       yesterday  john  deer-Indef  see-Decl
       'Yesterday, John saw a deer'.
(54b)  húuleesh  john  úuxa-m  íkaa-ʔ
       yesterday  john  deer-Indef  see-Q
       'Did John see a deer yesterday?'

Several other inflections can occur in the slot for -*k* and -*ʔ* at the end of the word. An -*h* in that position is an imperative marker, making a command. Crow also has an interesting pair of inflections called **switch reference markers**. In (55a), the suffix -*ák* is a so-called same subject marker (SS), meaning that the subject of the first clause ending in -*ák* will continue to be the subject in the following clause: the person coming, Martha, is the same as the person entering the house. In contrast, -*m* in (55b) is a different subject marker (DS): the subject of the following clause will switch from the subject of the clause ending in -*m*; that is, while Martha came, it was someone else who entered the house. Data from Graczyk (2007, 210).

(55a)  martha  huu-ák  ashé  biléeli-k
       martha  come-SS  house  enter-Decl
       'Martha came, and (Martha) entered the house'.
(55b)  martha  húu-m  ashé  biléeli-k
       martha  come-DS  house  enter-Decl
       'Martha came, and someone else entered the house'.

Some languages use **evidentials**, morphemes that express the speaker's feeling about the reliability or source of the information presented in the sentence. Tuyuca, a language in Brazil, has a set of evidential suffixes on the verb that specify where or how the speaker witnessed or otherwise obtained or deduced the information. Data adapted from Whaley (1997, 224, citing Palmer 1986, citing Barnes 1984).

(56a)  díiga       apé-wi
        soccer     play-Visual
        'He played soccer, I saw it'.
(56b)  díiga       apé-ti
        soccer     play-NonVisual
        'He played soccer; I heard it'.
(56c)  díiga       apé-yi
        soccer     play-Apparent
        'He played soccer. I didn't witness it, but I have evidence it happened'.
(56d)  díiga       apé-yigi
        soccer     play-Secondhand
        'He played soccer; someone told me'.
(56e)  díiga       apé-hiyi
        soccer     play-Assumed
        'He played soccer, it seems reasonable to assume'.

Languages without evidentials, such as English, must use roundabout phrases to express the nuances of information reliability. Tuyuca achieves the same effect with a short suffix.

## 4.5 Some Crosslinguistic Generalizations in Inflectional Morphology

The previous sections presented the use of inflections in a number of languages for various functions. The use of inflections across languages isn't random in the sense that some kinds of inflections are quite common, while others are rare. Here, we present a few crosslinguistic generalizations that have been claimed by linguists based on samples of languages. Most of the data are from the World Atlas of Language Structures Online by Dryer and Haspelmath (2013).

Case inflections on nouns seem to be relatively common, and they tend to be suffixes. In a sample of 1,031 languages, noun cases appear as suffixes in 452 languages (44%) and as prefixes in only 38 languages (less than 4%) (Dryer 2013b). Other strategies for indicating case, such as by tone or changing the stem, are extremely rare.

Morphology for marking tense and/or aspect on the verb is also quite common, again with a significant preference for suffixation. In a sample of 1,131 languages, 979 (almost 87%) have some sort of inflection to indicate tense and/or aspect (Dryer 2013c). Of those 979 languages, 820, or 84%, of them use affixation, and of those 820 languages that use affixes to mark tense/aspect, 667 (81%) use suffixing. English is a statistically normal language in this sense, marking tense as in *walk-ed*, not *\*ed-walk*.

To inflect for number (singular, plural, dual, etc.) on a noun, languages have a preference for affixation, in particular suffixation. In a sample of 968 languages with some form of plural markings, 639 (66%) use affixes as opposed to other devices such as tone or separate words (Dryer 2013d). Of those 639 affixing languages, 513 (80%) use suffixes. Again, English exemplifies the tendency: *cat-s*, not *\*s-cat*.

Indeed, inflections in general like to be suffixes, not prefixes. In a sample of 828 languages that have more than a "little affixation", 529 (64% of the sample) were either "strongly" or "weakly" suffixing, compared to 152 languages (18%) that were "strongly" or "weakly" prefixing (Dryer 2013a).

Evidential morphology is common. In a sample of 418 languages, 237 (57%) have some form of evidential marker (de Haan 2013). Of those 237 languages, 131 (55%) show evidentiality by an affix or clitic.

Person and number features are often assembled as portmanteau morphemes (Moravcsik 2013, 122, citing Plank 1999, 292). That is, a single morpheme is used to code person and number together rather than having separate morphemes – one for person and another for number. Spanish is a typical language in this regard. The suffix *-o* in the verb *hablo* ('I speak') corresponds to first person and singular as well as present tense.

## 4.6 Summary

This chapter presented inflectional morphology, which produces the various wordforms within a lexeme. Inflection, usually, but not always, involving prefixes and suffixes marks things such as number, gender, case, definiteness, tense, aspect, agreement and other items. Examples of some of the crosslinguistically common kinds of inflection were provided, along with some less common but, nonetheless, interesting inflectional morphology from various languages. The world's languages offer a wide range of how much inflection is available in any given language; some languages have very little inflection, while other languages have a lot, with a more-or-less range between those extremes.

## 4.7 Exercises

1. Regularizing Irregular English Plurals

    Most English nouns employ a regular plural inflection, which varies only phonologically depending on the last sound of the singular stem, as explained in Section 1.2. For example, the plural is [s] in words like *books*, [z] in words like *dogs* and [əz] in words like *churches*. There are still a good number of irregular plurals, i.e., plurals formed with something other than a [s], [z] or [əz], such as *mouse/mice*, *sheep/sheep*, *stimulus/stimuli*; sometimes there seems to be an option between a regular predictable plural and an irregular one, as in *index*, which pluralizes as both *indexes* and *indices*, and *person*, with *people* the most common plural but *persons* appearing in certain contexts.

    Over the course of the history of English, many formerly irregular plurals regularized. This was the case for *cow*, whose plural used to be *kine*. For the following words, indicate what the plural would be if the words used regular plurals. For example, if *woman* were a regular noun, the plural would be *woman[z]*. Caution: the focus is on the pronunciation, not the spelling. Hence, the expected plural would be *woman[z]*, even though it might be spelled *womans*.

    aircraft, analysis, bison, child, crisis, criterion, die, dwarf, elf, genus, goose, knife, loaf, nucleus, ox, phenomenon, series, swine, tooth, trout

2. Quiché

    Below is a partial paradigm of inflected forms for the word 'look for' in the Mayan language Quiché, also known as K'iche', which is spoken by a million people mostly in Guatemala. Given the words and their translations, deduce what the verbal stem is and what the subject and object pronoun prefixes are and how they attach to the verbal stem. The data are selectively chosen and slightly tweaked from Murdoch (1978). Spellings and some other details are simplified for the purposes of this exercise. In the glosses, read *you* as singular and *youall* as plural. While it is not crucial for identifying and solving the problem, the letter c is pronounced [k] and the letter j is pronounced like *j* in the English word *jury*, IPA [dʒ], not IPA [j].

1. catintzucuj'I look for you'.
2. cintzucuj'I look for him'.
3. cixintzucuj'I look for youall'.
4. ceintzucuj'I look for them'.
5. cinatzucuj'You look for me'.
6. catzucuj'You look for him'.
7. cujatzucuj'You look for us'.
8. ceatzucuj'You look for them'.
9. cinutzucuj'He looks for me'.
10. catutzucuj'He looks for you'.
11. cutzucuj'He looks for him'.
12. cujutzucuj'He looks for us'.
13. cixutzucuj'He looks for youall'.
14. ceutzucuj'He looks for them'.
15. xatintzucuj'I looked for you'.
16. xintzucuj'I looked for him'.

## 4.8 Arguable Answers

1. You could resort to an explicit rule, as was described in Section 1.3, but your intuitions should tell you what the regular form would be if the following has regular plurals.

   *aircraft* ⇒ *aircraft[s]*, instead of the usual irregular suffixless *aircraft*, though some speakers do use a regularized form.

   *analysis* ⇒ *analysis[əz]*, rather than the accepted irregular form *analys[iz]*.

   *bison* ⇒ *bison[z]*, not *bison*, although *bisons* may be a regular plural for some speakers.

*child* ⇒ *child[z]*, as children might sometimes say it.

*crisis* ⇒ *crisis[əz]*, similar to what would happen with *analysis*.

*criterion* ⇒ *criterion[z]*, instead of the Greek-based form *criteria*.

*die* ⇒ *die[z]*, and why in the world is it *dice* anyway?

*dwarf* ⇒ *dwarf[s]*, which had been a regular plural before it got confused with the pattern in *elf/elves*. The deregularized form *dwarves* is not uncommon. Certainly, my spellchecker is fine with it.

*elf* ⇒ *elfs*, not *elves*, pronounced with a [z]. If you're like me, you're pretty sure about *elf/elves*, but somewhat unsure about the plural of *dwarf*. My spellchecker doesn't like the faux regular form *elfs*

*genus* ⇒ *genus[əs]*, as opposed to the conventional plural *genera* in the field of biology.

*goose* ⇒ *goos[əz]*, again a form that children might say before they settle on *goose/geese*.

*house* ⇒ *hou[səz]*. This is a tricky one. The [əz] plural is already regular, so we don't have to regularize that part of the plural form. What we're regularizing is the final [s] in the stem, which, for some odd reasons, is commonly pronounced with a [z] before adding the plural.

*knife* ⇒ *knife[s]*, after all, the plurals of *reef* and *cuff* aren't *\*reeves* and *\*cuv[z]*.

*nucleus* ⇒ *nucleus[əz]*, not the occasional -*i* plural we got from Latin.

*ox* ⇒ *ox[əz]*, although most speakers are happy enough with *oxen*, even if it's not a terribly common word in any case.

*phenomenon* ⇒ *phenomenon[z]*, as with *criterion*, instead of the standard irregular *criteria*.

*series* ⇒ *series[əz]*. Maybe speakers didn't like an [s] and two [z] s in the same word, so we are stuck with the irregular *series/ series*.

*swine* ⇒ *swines*, not plural *swine*.

*trout* ⇒ *trout[s]*. It seems for fish and some mammals that are hunted, the uninflected plural is preferred, especially among those who fish and hunt.

## 2.  Quiché

There are entry routes into a morphological analysis, but the general strategy is always to match up each morpheme with a consistent piece of meaning in English. Some creative flexibility is needed because, often enough, the morphemes in another language don't always match up one-to-one. In the Quiché problem, it should be apparent that the Quiché verb matches up consistently with two pieces in English, *look for*. Morphology problems can also be challenging because of irregularities in both languages. However, here, the analysis is pretty straightforward.

Let's start with identifying the verb itself. Scanning down the words in 1–14, your first quick hunch might be that the constant throughout the Quiché wordforms in the paradigm is *c...tzucuj*, which matches the constant translation 'look(s) for'; *look/looks* is an English verb alternation, which we'll assume is irrelevant in the Quiché data. So, *c...tzucuj* could be the verb, with one or more infixes inserted between the initial *c* and *tzucuj* in the noncontiguous *c...tzucuj*. Not so fast though, as examples 15–16 begin with *x* instead of *c*; *c* is consistent with the data in the present tense, while *x* appears in the two past tense expressions. We surmise that the verb stem is *tzucuj* and that *c-* is a present prefix, while *x-* is a past prefix.

Because all the English translations have two pronouns, we'll look for what they correspond to in Quiché. For example, whenever *I* is the subject in English, Quiché uses the *in-* prefix.

Each English translation has a subject, the thing doing the looking, and an object, the thing being looked for. Ideally, we expect the subject and object to be reflected in the Quiché wordforms.

We're told to recognize without analyzing the initial *c-* prefix as some kind of verbal marker. Besides that, the constant form throughout the examples is *tzucuj*, so a good guess is that that must be the stem for 'look for'. The pronoun prefixes appear between the *c-* prefix and the verb stem.

When the subject is *I* in English, as in (1–4), the consistent prefix in Quiché is *in-*, immediately preceding the verbal stem. In (1), the Quiché piece not accounted for is *at-*, which apparently corresponds to the English object *you*. The morpheme *at-* corresponding to the object *you* also occurs in (10). So far, besides the verb and tense, it's reasonable to propose that *in-* is the prefix for a first-person singular subject, and *at-* is a prefix for the second-person singular object. The order of prefixes is tense-object-subject, in that order, followed by the verb stem.

If we're on the right path, all we have to do is identify the remaining morphemes. Whenever there's a *you* subject, as in (5–8), *at-* appears immediately preceding the stem. So, *at-* represents the second-person singular subject *or* object, identifiable as subject or object by its position. The same situation occurs with first-person singular. Besides being a subject prefix, *in-* is also a Quiché object, corresponding to *me*, in (5) and (9).

Things are falling into place. Looking at the other prefixes, we guess that *ix-* corresponds to the object *youall* in (3) and (13) and that *uj-* corresponds to *us* as the first-person plural object in (7) and (13). The prefix *e-* is *them*, the third-person plural object in (4) and (14). The third-person singular subject *he* shows up as the prefix *u-* in (9–14).

The only potentially confusing task is to find the third-person singular object corresponding to *him* in (2), (6) and (11). Because we've established a pronoun prefix order of object followed by the subject, in (2), for example, we expect to find something between present tense *c-* and the subject pronoun *in-*. Our conclusion is that Quiché doesn't mark the third-person singular object.

The Quiché verb is much more complex than suggested only by the data provided, and more data from the full verbal paradigm will provide more information about affixes and maybe the verb's structure. We may also have to reanalyze what's been proposed so far. For example, it turns out that the *j* at the end of the verb is not actually part of the verb stem but a separate morpheme. However, given the data we have above, we have a tentative morphological analysis.

| _Quiché Morpheme_ | _Meaning, Function_ |
|---|---|
| tzucuj | verb stem for 'look for' |
| c- | present prefix |
| x- | past prefix |
| in- | first-person singular subject, object |
| uj- | first-person plural object |
| at- | second-person singular subject, object |
| ix- | second-person plural object |
| u- | third-person singular subject |
| ∅- | third-person singular object |
| e- | third-person plural object |

<u>Morpheme Arrangement</u>
Tense-Object-Subject-Verb

# Chapter 5

# Derivation

## 5.1 Preliminaries

Let's reprise what isn't the longest word in English, the word we started with in Chapter 1. At the core of *antidisestablishmentarianism* is *establish*, which, by itself, functions as a verb. The bare wordform is *establish*, and there's a regular third-person singular present form, *establishes*, along with a regular past tense form, *established*. It can take the regular progressive ending, as in *The House is establishing an investigative committee*, and participle forms, as in *The House has established an investigative committee* and *An investigative committee was established by the House*, the perfect and passive, respectively. Through the inflectional morphology discussed in Chapter 4, that pretty much exhausts the wordforms in the verbal lexeme based on the root √ESTABLISH and provides strong evidence that the stem *establish* is a verb. Although we won't rule out all the other categories that it isn't, briefly, notice that it's not a noun because it doesn't work in noun contexts, such as **the establish*; the ungrammaticality of **very establish* and **This institution is more establish that than one* is strong evidence that it's not an adjective either.

(1)

| bare | 3 Sg Present | Past | Present Participle | Perfect/Passive Participle |
|------|-------------|------|-------------------|---------------------------|
| establish | establishes | established | established | established |

All these wordforms are used to express 'establishing' events, varying by tense, aspect, voice and agreement with the subject. In

DOI: 10.4324/9781003030188-5

contrast, *antidisestablishmentarianism* and any subwords, such as *establishment, disestablish,* etc., are not part of the verbal lexeme for *establish,* each subword being its own lexeme. For example, the noun *establishment,* morphologically derived from the verb *establish* with the suffix *-ment,* is a separate lexeme from *establish* and has its own set of lexeme wordforms, such as the singular and plural forms *establishment* and *establishments.* Further affixation derives other lexemes, including, of course, *antidisestablishmentarianism.* Unlike inflection, which gives us all the wordforms within a lexeme, the morphology for creating new lexemes allows speakers to create new words galore. The topic of this chapter, **derivational morphology**, can be defined as the morphology for creating new lexemes (Beard 1998, 44).

## 5.2 Creating Lexemes with Affixes: Case Study with -ness

Let's make a few observations about one particular derivational affix. The adjectives below can all take the suffix *-ness* to form corresponding nouns via derivational morphology.

(2a)    dull, wet, red, happy, heavy, obtuse, gregarious
(2b)    dullness, wetness, redness, happiness, heaviness, obtuseness, gregariousness

The suffixed forms differ from the stems they build on, i.e., are different lexemes. Not only have the categories changed from adjective to noun, but the meanings have changed in a systematic way. For one, the adjectives denote properties, but the nouns formed with the derivational suffix denote states of having those properties: *wet* refers to a certain property of having some significant component of liquid, while *wetness* denotes the state of having that property.

Observing the admittedly small sample of words above, we hazard a generalization that the suffix *-ness* forms nouns from adjectives. Put another way, the stems in *-ness* words tend to be nouns derived from adjectives and not from other categories, as attested in ungrammatical forms such as *\*go-ness, \*with-ness, \*the-ness* – it appears that *-ness* doesn't want to go on verbs, prepositions and determiners.

Now for some exceptions. Although preferring to attach to adjective stems, -*ness* has some flexibility in choosing other kinds of stems. On first glance, most of the examples below don't seem to work. But some of them sound okay, and once you let in a few, the others don't sound quite as bad. Maybe adding -*ness* to the preposition *with* is odd, at best, but suffixing -*ness* to the prepositional phrase *with it* seems to work. While *\*underness* and *\*toness* sound odd, *aboveness* seems not too bad. And if *aboveness* is possible, well then why not go back and rethink the grammaticality judgment of *underness*.

Again, out of the blue, we might not like *them-ness*, but on a parallel with *me-ness*, which Dixon (2014, 303) mentions as attested, *them-ness* begins to sound acceptable and, therefore, grammatical.

| (3) | V-ness: | *go-ness, *think-ness, *buy-ness |
| | P-ness | aboveness, *with-ness, with-it-ness, *under-ness, *to-ness, |
| | Conjunction-*ness* | *and-ness, *but-ness |
| | Complementizer-*ness* | *that-ness (*We think thatness you should apply for the job,) |
| | N-*ness* | dog-ness, cellphone-ness, |
| | D-*ness* | *the-ness, *much-ness, *this-ness |
| | Pronoun-*ness* | me-ness, them-ness |

In many cases, it may well be that the oddness or even ungrammaticality of some words stems from the form simply not being used much rather than an outright ban from the grammar. On the other hand, perhaps the data are telling us that while -*ness* can, indeed, be suffixed to various forms, it's most comfortable being appended to adjectives. So, we need not propose that -*ness* absolutely requires an adjective stem; rather, we can just observe that it canonically prefers to go on adjectives. Based on that assessment, we can propose that a -*ness* noun derives from an adjective, such as in (4a), and that the lexical entry for -*ness* must contain at least the information in (4b).

(4a)    [A-ness]$_{Noun}$
(4b)    -ness:    Suffix; /nɛs/; A-__ ⇒ N

We can also present the structural description as a morphological tree diagram, generally, and specifically for the word *wetness* as an example. Tree diagrams are visual alternatives to bracketing diagrams, as the one on the right side of example (5b). Both tree diagrams and diagrams show the composition of words into their parts and subparts.

(5a)

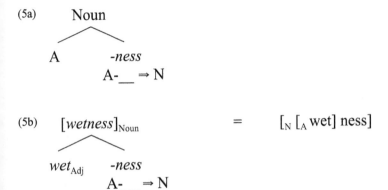

(5b)

The examples show the general pattern. Below *-ness* on the right branch of the tree is included its formula describing the environment it occurs in. The suffix goes in the gap indicated by underlining: ___. It attaches to the adjective stem on the left. The arrow says that the result of suffixing *-ness* to the adjective stem is a noun. The specific example shows the derivation of the noun form from the particular adjective *wet*. On the right is the bracketing diagram equivalent of the tree structure. It shows *wet* categorized as an adjective and the whole thing including the *-ness* suffix as a noun.

The data reveal that the general rule of *A-___* ⇒ *N* doesn't cover all appearances of the suffix *-ness*. In order to claim *A-___* ⇒ *N* we have put aside, for now, words such as *meness*. Further, given the smallness of the sample of *-ness* words we based the general rule on, we certainly can't rule out the possibility that we'll find more examples of *-ness* attaching to stems other than adjectives. See Exercise 1 at the end of the chapter to look at a large sample of *-ness* words to back up or contradict the claim that it generally goes on adjectives.

## 5.3 Derivational Affixes

English has a host of suffixes that derive lexemes from other lexemes. A few of the more common ones are listed below, with examples.

*-er* There are several related *-er* suffixes. One is added to verbs to derive a noun with the meaning 'someone or something that does or experiences the verb'. This agentive or experiencer *-er* occurs in *writer, walker, washer, thinker, walker, proofreader* and *camper* and is used to creatively make new nouns from verbs.

A related *-er* is added to bound roots, as in *astronomer*.

Another *-er* has the opposite function to indicate not the doer of a verb but the thing that is affected by the verb, as in *keeper*, for example, referring to a fish of sufficient size that you're allowed to keep as a catch.

Another *-er* goes on place nouns to indicate someone who lives in or comes from the place: *New Yorker, Newfoundlander* and *southerner*.

*-or* An alternative *-er* ending, which, despite the spelling difference, is pronounced the same as *-er*. It usually appears on Latin-based stems and often where the stem is somewhat opaque in meaning. Examples include *author, guarantor, spectator, actor* and *narrator*.

*-ize* Often suffixes to nouns to make verbs but can attach to other categories as well.

> *symbolize, scandalize, mobilize, materialize, legitimize, authorize*

*-less* Typically suffixes to nouns forming an adjective, indicating absence of the things denoted by the noun. However, other stems are possible, too. Some examples are *penniless, worthless, sightless* and *relentless*.

*-ish* A suffix often on adjectives of nouns, giving another adjective, meaning 'like, near'.

> *reddish, warmish, boyish, 8:30-ish, snobbish*

*un$_1$-* Meaning 'not', it prefixes to adjectives and gives us back an adjective, as in *unhappy* or *unfruitful*. It can also prefix participles that function as adjectives: *uneducated* and *uninspired*.

*un$_2$-* Not to be confused with *un$_1$-*, this prefix gives a verb that reverses the meaning of the stem verb. Words with this prefix include *unscrew, undo, uncover and untie*.

*re-* A prefix meaning something like 'again' that is added to verbs to get another verb, as in *redo, reinvent, repaint, reactivate* and *reapply*.

The following examples are arranged by the type of category change
with various derivational affixes. Note that some affixes do not change
the category of the stem.

(6)  Verb ⇒ Noun:     remov-**al**, protect-**ion**, revitaliz-**ation**, writ-**er**, endear-**ment**
     Verb ⇒ Adjective:  do-**able**, dismiss-**ive**, rest-**ing**
     Verb ⇒ Verb:     **un**-do, **re**-think, **dis**-inherit
     Noun ⇒ Noun:    king-**dom**, **anti**-pope
     Noun ⇒ Adjective:  girl-**ish**, health-**y**, kind-**ness**, child-**like**
     Noun ⇒ Verb:     computer-**ize**, **en**-tomb
     Adjective ⇒ Noun:  happi-**ness**, inan-**ity**, linguistic-**s**
     Adjective ⇒ Verb:  **en**-rich, light-**en**
     Adjective ⇒ Adj.:  blu-**ish**, **in**-hospitable, **super**-careful, **a**-political
     Adjective ⇒ Adverb: happi-**ly**

The list of derivational affixes in English is extensive. Many of them
have strong tendencies to behave in certain ways, like making adjectives out of nouns, but most have varying behavior to some degree.
Some are productive in that they can be freely used by speakers and
writers to create new words, such as the suffixes *-ness* and *-less.*
If I'm dismayed that a certain Italian restaurant doesn't have fet-
tuccine on the menu, I can complain that the restaurant is *fettuc-
cineless*, creating, as far as I know, a word that's not been attested
before. Many affixes may be frequent in that they appear on lots
of words but are of limited productivity. For example, *-th* appears
on some common words such as *truth, warmth, health, wealth,* but
the semantic relation between the stem and the derived word isn't
so clear, and speakers, for a long time, haven't been using it much
to make new words. Many suffixes are latched on to mysterious
stems because the words were borrowed into English as wholes.
While *comfortable* is transparently *comfort* suffixed with *-able,* the
stems in *possible, malleable* and *risible – poss-, malle-* and *ris- –* are
meaningless to English speakers. Words like these may appear to be
multimorphemic structures via derivational suffix with *-able/-ible,*
but, semantically, they're unanalyzable words. They may have been
morphologically and semantically more transparent in the original
languages that English borrowed from.

    For more complete lists of derivational affixes in English, see Sloat
and Taylor 1992 or many Googleable sites.

### *5.3.1 Zero Derivation*

Not all derivation requires an affix, and many English words lack any kind of affixation that marks them as obviously belonging to one category or other. For example, given the lack of inflection in English, many English nouns and verbs, at least in their bare form, aren't morphologically distinct. Take *walk*, for example. Is it a noun or a verb? In isolation, it's impossible to tell because neither has any derivational morphology. Even in the context of a sentence, there might not be any inflectional evidence either. In the sentences *Zak took the dog for a walk* and *Zak is going to walk the dog*, *walk* is morphologically identical. However, the syntactic context does inform us that *walk* is a noun in the first sentence and a verb in the second. That's because *walk*, preceded by the article *a* in the first sentence, is behaving like a noun, and in the second sentence, it's behaving like a verb as part of the infinitive form *to walk*.

Sometimes, cases of ambiguous word category have been analyzed as positing one word as more basic than the other. If we assume that *walk* is, at its heart, a verb, then the noun must be a derived form, though without any obvious derivational morphology, such as *-ment* or *-ation*. The conversion of a verb into a noun is described as adding a morpheme with no phonetic realization, just an abstract derivational morpheme that does what a pronounced derivational affix would do. This process, called **zero derivation**, also called conversion, is schematized below.

(7)

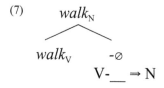

$$walk_N$$
$$walk_V \qquad -\varnothing$$
$$V\text{-}\underline{\quad} \Rightarrow N$$

The character $-\varnothing$ is the null sign, meaning that nothing is pronounced. But the derivation suggests that there is, nonetheless, some active morphology going on with this unpronounced bit of suffixation – a category change from verb to noun.

If, on the other hand, the basic form is held to be the noun, then a different null suffix does the opposite conversion.

(8)

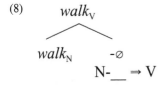

$$N\text{-}\_\_ \Rightarrow V$$

Of course, there's a problem, as it's something of a roll of the dice to decide which is more 'basic', *walk* the noun or *walk* the verb. One way out of this problem is to guess that there are at least two *walk*s in English – $walk_N$ and $walk_V$ – though having separate lexical entries might obscure the relationship of the two words as sharing some core meaning. Another way out of the problem is to use our idea of uncategorized roots in the lexicon. In this case, the words derive from a common $\sqrt{\text{WALK}}$. Whatever the precise theoretical account, zero derivation is common in English and other languages in that the same form can be of several categories.

### 5.3.2 Other Kinds of Derivation

There are a number of other fairly common ways to make new lexemes. While the preceding kinds of derivation via affixation are probably available in some form for speakers in languages around the world, some of the following depend on the language having a written form because they're related to spelling as well as spoken forms of the language.

An **abbreviation**, in a general sense, selects some of the letters of the spelling of a phrase, usually the initial letters of the words, which are then pronounced as a sequence of the letters. Common examples are *FBI* for *Federal Bureau of Investigation*, *BBC* for *British Broadcasting Corporation*, *U.N.* for *United Nations*. Abbreviations are common, and other examples include *FYI, OMG, WTF, CEO. DNA*, from *deoxyribonucleic acid*, goes inside one of the words to abbreviate one of its parts. Characters other than letters can be used as well, as in the name of the programming language *C++*, pronounced *C plus plus* [si plʌs plʌs]. Many, if not most, such abbreviations are unpronounceable as spelled out unless all the letters are pronounced: *BBC*, for example, has no vowels in the spelling and can't be pronounced [bbs] or [bbk]; rather, the pronunciation depends on pronouncing the letters as [bibisi]. Some abbreviations are used only in written contexts and never used as spoken forms, such as *tbsp* or *tbl* for *tablespoon* and *amt* for *amount*; a period may or may not be used after the abbreviation.

If the respelling is to be read as an ordinary word rather than as a sequence of pronounced letters, the result is an **acronym**. Acronyms are typically formed with the first letters of words in the expression. *UNESCO* is short for *the United Nations Educational, Scientific and Cultural Organization*. Often enough, the acronym is so prevalent and convenient that we may be unclear about its origin and what it stands for. Maybe some people know that *radar* is short for *radio detection and ranging*, but let's venture that hardly anyone can rattle off the top of their head that *scuba* is an acronym of *self-contained underwater breathing apparatus*. Going from under water to space, *NASA* is acronymic for *the National Aeronautics and Space Administration*, and one of NASA's Mars missions is *Insight*, which takes advantage of an already existing word while simultaneously standing for *interior exploration using seismic investigation, geodesy and heat transport*.

**Blends** are another kind of wordformation via abbreviation, often, though not always, based on spelling. As opposed to abbreviations and acronyms, which usually put together initial letters of a series of words, blends take chunks of words and put them together, though it's hard to tell if any particular blend is spelling-based or speech-based. A blend that's common in everyday speech is *smog*, formed from the *sm* at the beginning *smoke* and the *og* at the end of *fog*. Even if *smog* originates in spelling, it corresponds to syllable structure as well: *sm* being the syllable-initial part of *smoke*, while *og* is the syllable-final portion of *fog*. Referring to a foggy appearance stemming from atmospheric pollutants, *smog* has been around for more than a hundred years. A related example, *vog*, is used commonly in Hawaii, referring to volcano-related fog.

What is arguably a species of abbreviation in the general sense is **clipping**, which simply drops parts of words. *Delicatessen* appears in the Corpus of Historical English in the 1890s but, apparently, didn't get clipped into *deli*, at least in written records, until the 1960s. More recently, *mobile phone* got clipped to *mobile*. The person you're no longer married to or involved with is your *ex*, formerly known as your *ex-wife*, *ex-husband* or *ex-partner*. As opposed to other kinds of abbreviations, clipping usually leaves a recognizable residue of the original expression. Clippings can then be assembled into new lexemes. The clipped form *info* from *information* is joined with *tainment* from *entertainment* to form *infotainment*. The astronomy term *pulsar*, a kind of star, is a combination of *puls(ating st)ar*, presumably on analogy with *quasar*, from *quas(i stell)ar* (*radio source*).

**Backformation** is a kind of clipping of an affix from a word that often involves a change of category. The word *editor*, itself borrowed from Latin, appears in English in the mid-seventeenth century. As *-er/-or* is a common noun suffix added to verbs to make a noun, typically denoting someone or something that does the verb, as in *singer*, *heater* and *writer*, speakers, apparently, interpreted the *-or* as a nominalizing suffix and lopped it off to backform the verb *edit*. A few other back-formed verbs include *aggress* from *aggression*, *legislate* from *legislator* and *peddle* from *peddler*.

While many abbreviations, clippings, blends and acronyms are familiar to most speakers, many of them are specialized as parts of the jargon of specific business, academic, technological, governmental and social groups. You can easily Google for abbreviations in business, government and technology to find hundreds of mostly specialized forms used in those fields.

Though not involving morphology per se, an important source of new lexemes is **borrowing** from other languages. Probably all languages borrow words from other languages. English is a particularly prolific borrower, being heavily indebted to Latin and Greek as influential classical and religious languages and, especially, French because of the Norman invasion of English in the eleventh century and subsequent centuries of occupation and later influence of cultural contact with France. As a result, English today is filled with thousands of words of French origin. As an aside, 'borrowing' is a rather whimsical term, as languages don't return the words they borrow. We can say with regard to French, however, that in recent decades, much to the chagrin of l'Académie française, an official institution that tries to regulate the proper use and maintenance of French, the English-speaking world has lent lots of words to French, returning the favor after a millennium.

**Coinage** is the manufacture of lexemes, sometimes involving morphological processes and, these days, often appearing in the naming and marketing of products and companies, such as *Teflon* and *Kleenex*, both of which have expanded to become generic references in the language. Coinage is typically a very conscious and directed process. Science has often coined new words by combining roots and affixes, as in *proton*, *electron* and *neutron*, though, more recently, ordinary words have been commandeered with specialized meanings, such as *color*, *charm*, *spin*.

An amusing example of a failed coinage occurred in the early days of Enron Corporation, a defunct but once high-flying company with origins in the natural gas industry. A series of corporate mergers resulted in the clumsy name HNG/InterNorth, but HNG was already an abbreviation for Houston Natural Gas. A corporate consultant suggested *Enteron* as a trendy name by clip-combining *EN(ergy)* and *(in)TER(national)*, with *-ON* appended (because it sounded cool!). After printing 75,000 covers for an annual shareholders' report, the company learned that *enteron* is a medical term for the digestive tract. Not a great name for a gas company! Enteron was quickly shortened to *Enron*, which doesn't mean anything. The account of the naming of the company, which collapsed in financial shenanigans in 2001, is from Eichenwald (2005, 33–34) and McLean and Elkind (2003, 13–14).

Sometimes, things are named for people who discovered or otherwise explained them. Scientific words like *joule*, *curie*, *watt*, *fermi* honor the people who investigated the phenomena.

Urbandictionary.com is a convenient source for new words and expressions and expanded meanings for existing words.

### 5.3.3 Iterative Derivation

It's possible for derivation to be iterative, which is to say that derivation is repeatable and can involve more than a single derivational affix. With each affix, another stem is formed, and that stem can then receive another derivational affix. Iterative affixation results in additional structure. Until now, the examples of derived words have involved a stem and a single affix, resulting in a very simple structure that joins the two pieces, as in the previous example of *wetness*. When more than one affix is involved, the result is a more obviously hierarchical arrangement that reflects the structure and the word's meaning. That is, if you have a stem and two affixes, one affix applies first, creating a new stem, to which the other affix is added.

Consider the word *childlessness*. Besides the stem *child*, two suffixes can be identified, *-less* and *-ness*. The suffix *-less* attaches to the right of the noun stem *child* and yields an adjective meaning 'without a child', or a bit more naturally 'without children'. So far, we have the following structure.

(9)

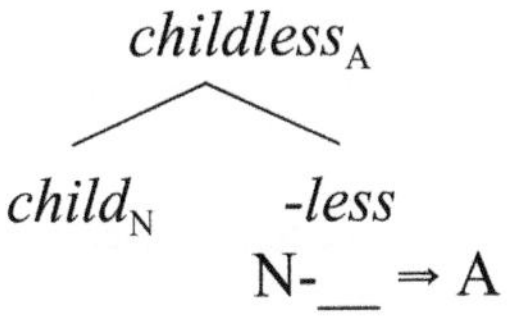

$childless_A$

$child_N$ — *-less*

N-__ ⇒ A

The adjective *childless* then becomes a stem for further derivational morphology, in this case, another suffix, *-ness*, which converts the adjective back into a noun.

(10)

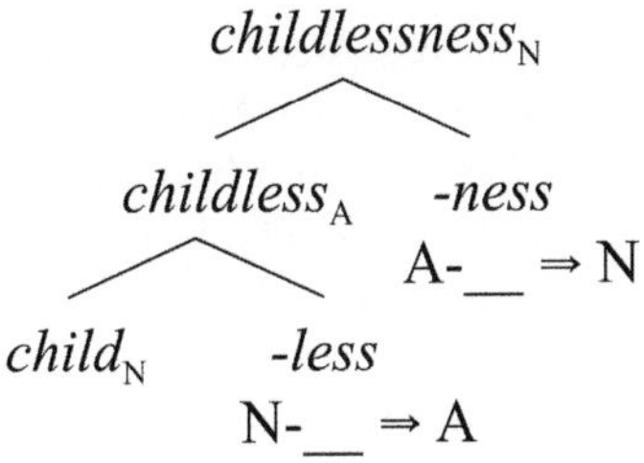

$childlessness_N$

$childless_A$ — *-ness*

A-__ ⇒ N

$child_N$ — *-less*

N-__ ⇒ A

With a string of suffixes, the structure builds up to the right, with the rightmost suffix at each stage dictating the category so far. In (10), *-less* takes the noun *child* and forms the adjective *childless*. The suffix to *-less*'s right then converts the adjective stem *childless* into a noun.

When derivational morphology involves both prefixes and suffixes, it's a little trickier to establish the order of affixation because, in principle, there's a choice of adding the prefix first, making the stem to which the suffix is added, or adding the suffix first, and then adding the prefix. Sometimes one is correct, but other times, either order of affixation is legitimate but with different meanings. As an example, let's look at *unscrewable* in some detail. The word has a prefix *un-* and a suffix *-able*. Recall from Section 5.3 that there are at least two *-un*s in English. The $un_1$- prefix, with a static meaning of 'not', attaches to an adjective stem and gives us back another adjective, as in *unhappy* ('not happy') and *uncertain* ('not certain'). In contrast, *un₂-*, meaning roughly 'reverse', has a more dynamic meaning and prefixes to verbs to give another verb, as in *undo* and *unlock*.

Assuming that the stem *screw* is a verb, then only *un₂-* can be prefixed to it, yielding the new stem [ᵥ un [ᵥ screw]], which is a verb. Now, the suffix *able-* ('able to be done') takes verbs and returns an adjective, giving us [ₐ [ᵥ un [ᵥ screw]] able] ('able to be unscrewed').

(11)

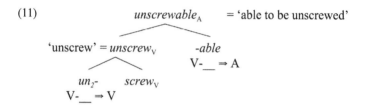

An alternative is to first suffix *-able* to the base stem *screw* to make the adjective [ₐ [ᵥ screw] able] ('able to be screwed'). Now that we have an adjective, only *un₁-* ('not') can be prefixed to it because *un₁-* prefixes to adjectives. So, we get [ₐ un [ₐ [ᵥ screw] able]], meaning 'not able to be screwed. The tree representation is in (12).

(12)     *unscrewable*ₐ     = 'not able to be screwed'

```
         un₁-              screwableₐ = 'able to be screwed'
      A-__ ⇒ A                  
                        screwᵥ      -able
                               V-__ ⇒ A
```

How to decide what attaches to what in a word like *ungraciousness*? There's no verb to be seen in this word, leaving *un₁-* ('not') as the only legitimate prefix, attaching to the adjective *gracious*. We've seen that *-ness* suffixes to adjectives to make nouns, so the only possible grammatical structure is [ₙ [ₐ un [ₐ gracious]] ness]. Right?

Yes, but it turns out that *un₁-* can sometimes attach to nouns as well, as in *unrest, unemployment, unacceptance. Unrest* refers to a condition of agitation, the opposite of *rest*, which, among other things, is a lack of agitation. *Unemployment* and *unacceptance* have the *un₁*- prefix meaning 'not'; clearly not the *un₂*- prefix, which would give us *unemploy* and *unaccept*, which don't seem to be English verbs.

What is the order of affixation in a word like *denationalization*? Let's work with a definition along the lines of 'the act of undoing the nationalized status of something', as in privatization of a state-run entity. The suffixes on *nation* add left-to-right; the question is where the prefix *de-* fits in. That is, does it prefix to *nation*, to *national*, to *nationalize* or to *nationalization*? The prefix *de-* has a range of meanings, often suggesting removal, reversal or negation: *declaw, decentralize, defreeze, detangle* and *deduct*. The meanings vary partly because sometimes the prefix was used by English speakers to derive words, as in *declaw* and *detangle*, but sometimes the prefix was borrowed as part of another word, as in *deduct* and *decrease*. However, there's a tendency for *de-*, when used productively, to attach to verbs to yield another verb meaning 'reverse, undo'. Now, within *nationalization*, without the prefix, we have *nation, national, nationalize* and *nationalization*. Only one of these, *nationalize* is a verb stem, so our best guess is that *nationalize* is what *de-* is prefixing to. Hence, we have the following derivation, slightly simplified for easier reading. The suffix *-al* makes the noun *nation* an adjective, *national*. Then *-ize* converts *national* into a verb, *nationalize*. Now the verb-seeking *de-* prefixes to the verb *nationalize*, the only place it can attach, to make another verb, *denationalize*. Finally, *-ation*, a frequent enough suffix, takes the verb *denationalize* and gives us a noun.

(13)

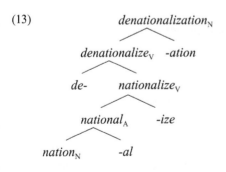

One note on sound. You might have noticed that the pronunciation of the vowel in *nation*, with an [e] sound, becomes [æ] in the derived forms. There's nothing regular about this in the sense that, specifically, [e] vowels become [æ] vowels during derivation or, generally, that vowels change in any systematic way in derivations. It's just a quirk of the history of English that the vowel changes between *nation* and its derivatives. Note there's no vowel change in pairs like *person/ personal*, *scribe/scribal*.

That said, as a side observation, there is set of derivations that involve systematic vowel changes.

(14)  [i]/[ɛ]      ser**e**ne/ser**e**nity, comp**e**te/comp**e**titive
      [e]/[æ]      prof**a**ne/prof**a**nity, in**a**ne/in**a**nity
      [ai]/[ɪ]     der**i**ve/der**i**vative, mal**i**gn/mal**i**gnant
      [au]/[ʌ]     den**ou**nce/den**u**nciation, prof**ou**nd/prof**u**ndity

The alternations go by the name trisyllabic laxing – trisyllabic because the affected vowel is often followed by three syllables, and laxing, because there's a change from a tense vowel in the stem (e.g., [i], [e], [ai], [au]) to a lax counterpart ([ɛ], [æ], [ɪ], [ʌ]) in the derived form. There are plenty of exceptions in which the vowel doesn't change, as in *obese/obesity* and *hyphen/hyphenate*, and both the stem and derived forms are words; that is, trisyllabic laxing is, at most, very marginally productive. We simply memorize both forms and are left with a curious pattern. In fact, trisyllabic laxing has its roots in vowel changes that occurred between about 600 and 400 or so years ago in the history of the English language.

### 5.3.4 Derivation in Other Languages

Derivational morphology of some sort is available in perhaps nearly all languages. Certainly, it's crosslinguistically more common than inflectional morphology. Romance languages have many affixes that are recognizable to English speakers because of the Latin influence on the English lexicon. Romance languages inherited these affixes directly from their mother language; English got them either directly through borrowing from Latin or borrowing from the daughter languages. Among the similar derivational morphemes are the nominalizing *-(a)* *tion* suffix in French, which shows up in Spanish as *-ación* and in Italian as *-azione*.

It's not surprising to see some similar derivational morphology between, say, French and English: they're both Indo-European languages and have been affected by extensive borrowing through language contact. Looking at a completely unrelated language, we observe that the Siouan language Crow has a number of affixes whose semantic contribution is fairly transparent. The suffix *-kaata* is a diminutive deriving, for example, *áashkaata* ('stream or creek') from *áashi* ('river'); as a result of the suffixation, the final vowel in the stem *áashi* drops off (Graczyk 2007, 45). The prefix *ak-* roughly corresponds to the commonest use of the English suffix *-er* on verbs, signaling 'one who does the verb'. Where English has *writer*, *runner*, *thinker*, Crow has *ak-disshí* ('one who dances') (Graczyk 2007, 47).

## 5.4 Compounds

A simple way to make new lexemes is to make **compounds** by combining noun, verb and adjective roots. As an example, the word *bluebird* results from combining *blue* and *bird*. Compounding is a very common type of derivational morphology crosslinguistically, and, perhaps, all languages have some type of compounding, even if they don't have much in the way of other kinds of morphology. According to some linguists (e.g., Jackendoff 2002; Progovac 2015), compounding could be a relict or fossil of the earliest kinds of protolanguage when humans hadn't yet developed full grammatical language. Prelinguistic humans likely had a lexicon of sorts – even nonhumans have vocabularies of sounds and behaviors attached to certain meanings. But early humans are hypothesized to have lacked the grammatical means for making new words and sentences out of their early lexicons. What they could do, it is argued, is combine at least two items from their lexicon with some kind of compositional meaning.

Compounds are structured in various ways. Perhaps the most common compounds, at least in English, are compound nouns. The example above, *bluebird*, is a compound noun comprising a head, *bird*, and a modifier, *blue*. The **head** of the compound, usually on the right edge of the compound, dictates the category of the compound: because *bird* is typically a noun, the whole compound is a noun. As for meaning, the head denotes the broad class of objects, which is then restricted by the modifying portion of the compound. That is, a bluebird is a kind of bird. Because not all blue birds are bluebirds (for example, blue jays) and not all bluebirds are particularly blue (females and juveniles), blueness is neither a sufficient nor necessary property for inclusion in the class of bluebirds, but the expression *bluebird* does narrow down the class of birds by providing a salient property of blueness, at least for adult males. If *bluebird* doesn't unambiguously identify all the individuals that are bluebirds, it does, nonetheless, get us in the ballpark of bluebirds.

Compounds such as *bluebird* are **endocentric**, meaning that the head appears as part of the compound. Like *bluebird*, *washcloth*, *gig economy*, *clock tower*, *computer program* and *greenhouse* are all endocentric compound nouns. Note that the modifiers in these compounds seem to be a verb, noun, noun, noun, adjective, respectively. However, it's not always obvious that the modifier is a verb or noun or adjective, and, as we saw in Section 1.3, there's evidence that the modifier doesn't have a particular category. In *bluebird*, while *blue* seems to be an adjective because, in other contexts, it is an adjective, inside the compound, it doesn't behave like an adjective. For example, *\*bluerbird* with the comparative of *blue* doesn't seem to work in English.

Not all compounds have semantic heads to indicate the thing we're modifying. *Numbskull* doesn't refer to a kind of skull; rather, a numbskull is a kind of person. *Lightyear* is not a kind of year or any kind of time unit but is a measure of distance. Such compounds are called **exocentric**.

We'll mention one other broad category of compound that doesn't involve a kind-of relationship. **Coordinate compounds** (or coordinative compounds) such as *producer-director* suggest not a kind of director but, rather, someone who's both a producer and a director.

Compounds can, and do, join different kinds of roots, and the heads can be any lexical category, such as nouns, verbs and adjectives. For convenience, we'll momentarily identify the modifier as having the category that it usually has. In this sense, we can say that *bluebird* is an adjective-noun compound. With that in mind, we can combine various categories of modifier with various categories of head, though not all combinations occur with equal frequency. Noun-noun compounds include the already mentioned *gig economy* and *clock tower*. Examples of adjective-noun compounds are *greenhouse* and *fast track*, while *flyboy* looks like a verb-noun compound. *Upload* involves a prepositional modifier with a verb head and *into* is a compound preposition made of two prepositions.

The morphemes going into compounds can be free or bound. The examples in this section, so far, involve free morphemes, but bound morphemes are quite common in compounds. Recall that bound morphemes are those that don't stand alone as independent words. *Astro-* is a bound morpheme that can combine with *-naut*, another bound morpheme, to form *astronaut*. *Crypto-* is usually a bound morpheme meaning something like 'hidden or secret'. It's related to the free morpheme *crypt*, which refers to an underground area in a church for burial, and the derived adjective *cryptic*, meaning 'mysterious, secret or hidden'. Recently, the morpheme appears frequently in the word *cryptocurrency*. Interestingly, *crypto(-)* is something like *quasi(-)*, which we discussed in Section 1.4 as being free/bound-indeterminate. Within the space of four paragraphs *The New York Times* (May 13, 2022, 1) spelled *cryptocurrency* as one word, *crypto* as an independent word and *crypto companies* as two words; later in the article, we read *crypto billionaires* and *crypto platforms*. We could hypothesize that the free-looking *crypto* in such examples is a clipped form of *cryptocurrency*. In any case, the take-home point, again, is that the difference between free morphemes and bound morphemes, especially with regard to compounds, is not black and white.

So far, the structure of compounds is simple: XY, where Y is the morphological and often the semantic head of the compound. But, in principle, there's no limit on the number of morphemes that go into a compound. And, as compounds get longer, the structure becomes more evident in terms of what's modifying what. A plastic bird bath could be a bird bath that's made of plastic, as in (14a), or a bath for plastic birds, as in (14b). Both are morphologically and semantically plausible, although the example in (14a) is, practically speaking, the much more likely analysis and interpretation.

(14a)    plastic [bird bath]
(14b)    [plastic bird] bath

In (14a), the head is *bird bath*, itself a compound of *bird* and *bath*, and the result is a kind of bath. In (14b), the head is simply *bath*, modified by the compound *plastic bird*, where *bird* is the head; the meaning is a kind of bath.

One more compounding type is the **synthetic compound**. A synthetic compound can be described as including a head that's derived from a verb and a modifier that is an argument of the verb; usually the argument is a direct object. Typically, the *-er* suffix, usually indicating someone who does the verb, is added to the verb to derive a noun that heads the compound, for example *hunter*, *writer* and *watcher*, derived from *hunt*, *write* and *watch*. Add the modifiers, and we have *duck hunter*, *paperback writer* and *bird watcher*, where *duck*, *paperback* and *bird* are the objects of the verbs. It's not entirely clear whether synthetic compounds should be analyzed as, for example, [*duck hunt*]-*er* or [duck][hunt-er]. However, V-*er* words, such as *writer*, are quite common while N-V compounds, such as *paperback writer*, are not. So, one could argue that it's more natural to first form the V-*er* head and then compound this with the object-like modifier.

## 5.4.1 Compound or Phrase?

We've claimed that *bluebird* is a compound word, as opposed to *blue bird*, which is two words. In fact, *blue bird* is a noun phrase comprising the adjective *blue* and the noun *bird*. In *bluebird*, *bird* is the head of the compound while, analogously, *bird* is the head of the phrase *blue bird*. But why do we think *bluebird* and *blue bird* are two different structures, the former at word level and the latter at phrase level? Certainly not because of length, as they both contain two morphemes. Yet, if the claim is that these are two different structures, then there must be some criteria for making the claim. Positing two different structures stems, partly, from linguists' penchant to categorize things as noun or verb, adjective or noun, question or statement, inflection or derivation, when it's often difficult or impossible to make clean categorizations. The same applies here. Yet, while it's difficult to sharply differentiate between what's a word and what's a phrase, there are criteria for determining whether something tends toward wordness or phraseness. The following is a partial list of criteria.

First, speaker intuitions about language are sometimes informative but often unreliable. While some speakers feel that *bluebird* is a single word, others will wonder if it's really two words.

Second, orthography, as we've seen, can be suggestive but inconsistent. Dictionaries list *dragonfly* as one orthographic word but *horse fly* as two, although some searching on the internet quickly finds the variations *horsefly* and *horse-fly*. There doesn't seem to be a clear reason why *dragonfly* is be spelled rather consistently as one word but not *horse fly*. Where English is consistent is in pretty much limiting to only two the number of roots it spells as a single uninterrupted word. In spelling, English has *waxwing* and *cedar waxwing* but not *\*cedarwaxwing* and *hummingbird* and *rufous hummingbird* but not *\*rufoushummingbird*. In contrast, German, with the same compounding grammar as English, happily strings three, four or more words without orthographic spacing. Examples are *Blatthornkäfer* ('leafhornbeetle'), *Bruttoinlandsprodukt* ('grossdomesticproduct') and *Arbeiterunfallversicherungsgesetz* ('workersaccidentinsurancelaw'). Despite the inconsistencies within English and differences in spelling with German, English orthography is, nonetheless, informative with regard to compounding. While we can't tell from spelling whether two English words spelled separately make up a compound word or a phrase, when something is spelled as one unit, it's probably a compound not a phrase.

Semantics provides another criterion for distinguishing compound words from phrases. In a phrase, the modifier contributes its meaning to the meaning of the phrase; that is, the phrase is semantically compositional. However, compounds are less semantically compositional because the modifier can be pretty wiggly about its semantics. A blue bird is blue; it sounds contradictory to assert that a certain blue bird isn't blue. But a bluebird need not be blue, as it's hardly a contradiction to point out that some bluebirds aren't blue.

Phonology also provides some clues for distinguishing phrases from compounds, one of which is placement of main stress. **Stress** is relative strength in loudness, the volume of your voice, and pitch, how high in pitch your voice is. A stressed syllable is usually louder and higherpitched than adjacent syllables with less stress. Using capital letters to indicate stressed syllables, the noun *REcord* has stress on the first syllable while the verb *reCORD* is stressed on the second syllable. Individual nouns, verbs, adjectives and often prepositions usually have a single main stress. Therefore, a phrase made of two words will have two main stresses, as in *BLACK BIRD*. But when the components make up a single word, as in a compound, that single word will have one main stress, usually toward the front of the word in simple compounds, with the other syllable(s) relatively less stressed, as in *BLACKbird*. But caution is in order because not all compounds follow this pattern. For example, *BLACK HOLE* seems in some ways to be a compound, but Youtube videos show astronomers, at least American astronomers, pronouncing it with two stresses. Still, the stress criterion is informative because we can say that if, for example, a two-part structure has a single stress, especially if the stress is on the first syllable, we have evidence of a compound, i.e., a single word. But if a two-part structure has two stresses, we don't know for sure by that criterion alone whether we're dealing with a single-word compound or a multiword phrase.

Word-level effects on phonology occur in other languages as well. Similar to English compounds retaining a single stress is the behavior of accent in Crow, in which an accented syllable is realized as having a higher pitch. Most morphemes that correspond to nouns, verbs and adjectives have a single accent specified as part of the pronunciation of a word. Placement of the accent is important because it can be used to distinguish words. For example, in (15a), the first syllable is accented (marked with ´ above the vowel of the syllable), while in (15b), the accent is on the second syllable. Data are from Graczyk (2007, 20).

(15a)  *chía* 'white'
(15b)  *chiá* 'extinguish'

In compounding, similar to the situation in English, only one accent remains in the pronunciation, usually the first one, as in (16). Data are from Graczyk (2007, 21).

(16)  íaxchi 'reins' + úuwata 'metal'    ⇒    íaxchuuwata 'bridle'

In the case of (16), the final vowel in *íaxchi* also disappears.

Vowel harmony is a process whereby vowels in a word must be somehow similar. Examples are the Turkish words in (17), in which the pronunciation of the vowel in the plural suffix varies depending on the vowels in the noun stem. Data are adapted from Moravcsik (2013, 154).

(17)   çocuk-lar 'child-PL'
       köpek-ler 'dog'PL'

We won't go into the precise rules of vowel harmony in Turkish. Suffice it to say that the plural is *-lar* or *-ler*, depending on the vowels that precede it. The important point here is that this harmony only takes place within words: if harmony occurs, then what's affected is a word, for example, compounds; if harmony doesn't occur, that means you're dealing with more than one word.

A final clue to mention for telling a compound from a phrase is that the modifying element in a compound is usually itself not modifiable. Starting with the phrase *blue bird*, there's no problem adding the word *very* to modify *blue* to create the phrase *very blue*. In turn, *very blue*, as a whole, modifies the noun *bird*.

(18)   [very blue] bird

However, if instead of the phrase *blue bird* we have the compound *bluebird* (which, by the way, has the compound stress pattern *BLUEbird*), it's very odd to try to modify the modifier *blue* inside the compound: *\*very bluebird*.

The above criteria can help distinguish compounds from phrases, although it's important to keep in mind that there are no surefire tests. The following table summarizes criteria for telling a compound from a phrase, keeping in mind that no single criterion is foolproof.

(19) **Properties of Compounds v. Phrases**

| Property | Caution |
| --- | --- |
| i. Speaker intuitions. Speakers think *bluebird* is a single word. | From a morphologist's analytical point of view, speaker intuitions are inconsistent and unreliable. |
| ii. Orthography. *Bluebird* is spelled as a single word. | Spelling conventions are inconsistent. A single orthographic word is probably a good indicator of wordhood, but spacing as two or more words is not a good indicator of nonwordhood. |

iii. Semantics. Compounds are more likely than phrases to lose their strict semantic compositionality. A bluebird isn't necessarily blue, while a blue bird is blue.

Many compounds are transparently compositional. The word *black* in *black hole* does make a clear contribution to the meaning of the whole.

iv. Phonology. Word-level phonology, for example, word stress, is reflected in compounds: *BLUEbird* is a compound while *BLUE BIRD* is a phrase.

Again, there are many exceptions. Many expressions that are compounds by some tests fail this particular test. *BLACK HOLE* is a compound despite the two strongly stressed syllables.

v. Modifier's modifier. While modifiers in a phrase are modifiable, e.g., *very blue bird*, modifiers in a compound aren't easily modified, as in *\*very bluebird*.

A somewhat reliable test in simple compounds, but it doesn't hold as obviously in some other compounds such as *red-winged blackbird*.

The fact that it's difficult to classify compounds and phrases into two distinct morphosyntactic structures could mean at least two things. First, perhaps morphologists haven't yet identified with adequate precision the right set of criteria for telling a compound from a phrase. Second, it might be that, while any particular expression is more or less compound-like or phrase-like, there isn't a clean distinction. It's common in linguistics to find that there simply isn't a sharp boundary between purported categories.

## 5.5 Incorporation

One more example of derivational morphology is incorporation. While there are many kinds of incorporation with various analyses presented by linguists, below is discussed a very basic kind of noun incorporation. **Noun incorporation** is when an otherwise independent noun is absorbed by a verb, effectively resulting in the creation of a new verb. In some ways, noun incorporation, or something like it, occasionally occurs in English. The verb *plow* is usually transitive, taking the direct object *snow* as in (20a). An alternative sentence with more or less the same meaning is in (20b), in which *snow* appears in another position before the verb, usually analyzed as actually inside the verb.

(20a)   They had to [<sub>Verb</sub> plow] snow all morning
(20b)   They [<sub>Verb</sub> snowplowed] all morning

In (20b), by virtue of noun incorporation, the transitive verb *plow* has been converted into an intransitive verb *snowplow*.

This kind of morphology is not terribly common in English, and not all morphologists would call it true noun incorporation. A clearer example of what's usually accepted as a standard kind of noun incorporation comes from the Iroquoian language Mohawk. In example (21), from (Baker 1988), the direct object *ne owira'a* ('the baby') appears as the direct object to the right of the verb *nuhwe's* ('likes'). We know that *ne owira'a* ('the baby') is a direct object because of the agreement prefix *shako-*. The gloss in the second line of (21) tells us that the subject is a third-person masculine thing, *sak*, and that there's a feminine object, *ne owira'a* ('the baby'). Therefore, the verb is transitive, with both a subject and an object.

(21)   sak      shako-                        nuhwe's   ne    owira'a
       Sak      3.Subj.Masc/3.Obj.Fem-        like      the   baby
       'Sak likes the baby'.

The sentence in (22) is the noun-incorporated version of the sentence in (21), with the morpheme for 'baby' becoming part of the verb and no longer an independent direct object.

(22)   sak                    ra-              wira-     nuhwe's
       Sak                    3.Subj.Masc-     baby-     like
       'Sak likes the baby'.

The object is now morphologically attached to the left of the verb in a different form. This is not simply variation in where the object appears for two reasons. First, (22) uses a truncated form for 'baby', *wira-*, as opposed to *owira'a* in (21). Second, the article *ne* that appears in (21) is dropped in (22). Third, the prefix in (22) is *ra-*, which agrees ONLY with the subject *sak*, not with the object, because there is no object: the verb *ra-wira-nuhwe's* ('baby like') has become intransitive. So, what has happened between (21) and (22) is the creation of a new lexeme; the intransitive verb 'baby-like' with an incorporated noun object.

The example in (23) shows that trying to supply (22) with a semantically plausible object results in ungrammaticality because 'baby-like' is intransitive and doesn't want a direct object.

(23)    *sak        mari        ra-                        wira-nuhwe's
        Sak         Mary        3.Subj.Masc-               baby-like
        Intended: 'Sak baby-likes Mary'

The Mohawk example roughly parallels the English *snowplow* example in (20). The verb *plow*, by itself, is transitive, with a subject and object, as in *I'm plowing snow*. But when *snow* becomes part of the verb *snowplow*, we end up with an intransitive verb that prefers NOT to have an object. It's fine to say *I snowplowed*, but *I snow-plowed the snow* is awkward, if not ungrammatical.

## 5.6 Putting Together Derivation and Inflection

Recall the basic distinction between derivation and inflection: derivation results in new words or lexemes, while inflection accounts for the wordforms within a lexeme, which means that the two kinds of morphology can work together. We can derive the lexeme *snowplow* from *snow* and *plow* and then inflect it for past tense to get *snowplowed*. In example (22), the lexeme *wira-nuhwe's* ('baby like') is formed through derivational morphology and then gets the third-person masculine agreement prefix through inflectional morphology.

Some languages can go to great lengths to mix derivation and inflection and come up with long complicated words. A careful look at a word that corresponds to a longish complex sentence in English is instructive. Let's consider (24) from Crow, taken from Gracyzk (2007, 200) and a favorite among Crowologists.

(24)    ak-dii-ammalapáshkuua-ss-aa-lee-waa-chiin-moo-k
        Rel-2B-Billings-Goal-Port-go-1A-look.for-Incl-Decl
        'We'll look for someone to take you to Billings'.

As always, the third line provides a natural sounding translation, but if the word is literally translated, it would come out something like

(25)   ak-dii-ammalapáshkuua-ss-[aa-lee]-waa-chiin-moo-k
       someone.who-you-Billings-to-[take]-I-look.for-and.you-Statement

Let's carefully investigate how this long Crow verb is put together. The core of the expression is the verb *chiin* ('look for'), the third morpheme from the right. While the English translation suggests future tense, Crow has no future tense in its grammar, and the future meaning is simply inferred.

The English translation tells us that the subject corresponds to *we*. In Crow, this is made of two pieces, the prefix *waa-* immediately preceding the verb and a suffix *-moo* immediately after the verb. *Waa-* is glossed as 1A, which mnemonically can be thought of as 1 for first-person and A for agent, someone who does the looking. The suffix *-moo* is a kind of plural called inclusive. Recall that inclusive means that the speaker and the person they're talking to will together look for something. This Crow construction for 'we' is more precise than English *we*, which is ambiguous between meaning 'me and you' or 'me and someone else' or 'me and you and someone else'. What we have so far is *waa-chiin-moo*, 'you and me look for'.

What you and me are looking for is someone to take you to Billings. 'Someone' is taken care of with the first morpheme on the left, *ak-*. Technically, *ak-* is a relative pronoun, something like *who*, but *someone* works better as a natural-sounding English translation. It heads the relative clause corresponding to English 'someone who will take you to Billings'.

The second morpheme on the left, *dii*, is glossed as 2B, which means second person and, because there's no additional plural marker, *dii* is interpreted specifically as second-person singular. The B means it's not the agent A and indicates that *dii* ('you') is being acted on, not the one acting. That is, *dii* ('you') is the one to be taken to Billings.

Speaking of Billings, a city in Montana outside the Crow Reservation, that's the morpheme *ammalapáshkuua*. The gloss simplifies and overlooks that *ammalapáshkuua* itself is morphologically complex, meaning something like 'place where they cut logs'. The following morpheme *-ss* is glossed as goal and basically corresponds to the English preposition *to*. When English speakers say *to Billings*, Crow speakers say something like *Billings to*.

The meaning of *go* is carried in the Crow verb *lee*, the fifth morpheme from the right. The preceding *aa-* makes an intransitive motion verb transitive. Here, it effectively converts intransitive *lee* ('go') into *aa-lee* ('take').

The result so far is *ak-dii-ammalapáshkuua-ss-aa-lee-waa-chiin-moo*. This also can be translated as 'We'll look for someone to take you to Billings', but Crow grammar requires a final piece to indicate whether the expression is a statement, a question, a command or certain other options. The final *-k* suffix makes the sentence declarative – a simple statement.

Summarizing, here's a list of the morphemes in the order of left-to-right appearance with their contributions to the word.

(26) **Morphemes in the Word in (24)**

| | |
|---|---|
| ak | Relativizer, roughly translates as 'someone who' |
| dii | 'you' |
| ammalapáshkuua | 'Billings' |
| ss | 'to' |
| aa | Transitivizer, makes the following verb for 'go' into 'take' |
| lee | Literally 'go', but when preceded by *aa* means 'take' |
| waa | First person, doer of the action, indicates who will look for something |
| chiin | 'look for' |
| moo | Pluralizes *waa* to include both the speaker of the sentence and the person being spoken to |
| k | Declarative marker, indicates a statement |

It might be asked, well, how do we know this is a single word? It's spelled as one word because Graczyk and other researchers, such as Wallace (1993), have argued that such constructions are single words, not only including various inflections but also incorporation, discussed in Section 5.5. Perhaps the best indicator of wordhood is phonology. Note that the part that means 'Billings', *ammalapáshkuua*, is orthographically marked with a single accent. Because Crow words have, at most, a single accent, the construction put together with incorporation and various inflections must be a single word. That reasoning holds if phonological words match morphological words. The details are involved, and, in the end, we can't be sure that we are dealing with a single word. In fact, Golston et al. argue that it's not and that, despite appearances, things like relative clauses can't be incorporated.

## 5.7 Derivation v. Inflection

As earlier stated, derivation makes new lexemes, while inflection makes different wordforms within a lexeme. The distinction is somewhat clear in English, but questions do arise in English not to mention in other languages. For example, -ed can be added to any regular verb to form the past tense form, and -ed is clearly an inflection. But affixes such as re- can also be added to most verbs with a consistent meaning of 'again, repeated', just as -ed consistently indicates the past. But re- is considered derivational, while -ed is inflectional. The question arises whether there are any criteria for deciding what's an inflectional affix and what's a derivational affix. In fact, there are a number of general properties proposed by morphologists to distinguish these two kinds of wordformation. Here we'll present a few of the more important ones.

Starting with semantics, derivational morphology provides words with meanings that are relatively clear, concrete and able to refer to things and events in the world, while the contribution of inflectional morphology is more abstract, grammatical and language-internal. The derived word *motherly* has a pretty clear meaning of 'like a mother', with each of the morphemes making a semantic contribution to the whole word. In contrast, the inflection suffix -s on the verb *arrives* doesn't have a meaning per se; it's just a grammatical marker that says the verb agrees with a third-person subject.

Another point about semantics is that inflections don't fundamentally alter the meaning of the base, while derivations often do change the core meaning. The inflected forms *ride, rode, ridden* all somehow refer to riding events. However, in deriving *writer* from *write*, the meaning changes from an action to a person who does that action.

Third, inflections are required in certain syntactic contexts in a way that derivation isn't. The suffix -s is required on English verbs in the present tense when the subject is third-person singular. Similarly, in the Crow examples in the previous section, the person marker *waa-* is required when the first-person subject of the verb is the doer of the verb. On English nouns, when referring to more than one individual, a plural marker is usually required, as in *cats, pencils, suffixes*. However, there's no context that requires a form made through derivational morphology. For example, derivational suffixes such as *-ion* and *-ation* form nouns such as *institution* and *institutionalization*, but a verb never cares what particular morphological form the subject noun takes; bare nouns, acronyms and various derived forms are all fine as the subject of *is being investigated* in (27).

(27)    Damien/The ISI/The institute/The institution/The institutionaliza-
        tion is being investigated

Fourth, inflections never change the category of the base, while deriva-tions may or may not change category. So, *sing*, *sings*, *sang*, *sung* and *singing* are all verbs, and in Italian *canto*, *canti*, *canta*, *cantiamo* and many other forms are all forms of the verb 'sing', with various suf-fixes for who's doing the singing, when the singing is being done, etc. Derivation, however, may, but doesn't have to, change the category; *silly* is an adjective while *silliness* is a noun, but the noun *serf* retains its noun category in the derived form *serfdom*.

Fifth, generally, inflections are very consistently applied through a lexeme and leave no gaps in wordforms. The sample verbs in (28) all have a base form: third-person singular present form, past form, parti-ciple form and -*ing* form. There are no gaps in the paradigms, and the inflections are fully productive throughout the paradigm.

(28)    **Complete Verb-Inflection Paradigms**

|  | Base | Third sg -*s* | Past -*ed* | Participle -*en* | Participle -ing |
|---|---|---|---|---|---|
| Inflection | walk | walks | walked | walked | walking |
| Inflection | bite | bites | bit | bitten | biting |
| Inflection | cut | cuts | cut | cut | cutting |
| Inflection | talk | talks | talked | talked | talking |

Derivation typically leaves lots of gaps – forms that happen not to be words in English, though, of course, they could be. So, while there are the derived forms *profession* and *professor*, English happens to lack *professive*, although given *regressive*, we might expect *professive* to be a fine English word. Obviously, such suffixes are not completely productive.

(29)    **Incomplete Derivational Paradigms**

| Suffixes | Base | -*ion* | -*or*/-*er* | -*ive* | -*ful* |
|---|---|---|---|---|---|
| Derivation | profess | profession | professor |  |  |

| Derivation | regress | regression | | regressive | |
|---|---|---|---|---|---|
| Derivation | stress | | stressor | | stressful |
| Derivation | mess | | | | |
| Derivation | | mission | | missive | |
| Derivation | impress | impression | | impressive | |
| Derivation | aggress | aggression | aggressor | aggressive | |

One other property to mention is the linear position of the affix relative to the base. A crosslinguistic tendency is for derivational affixes to locate close to the base, inside inflectional affixes. Assuming a base adjective *internal*, the suffix *-ize* gives us a verb, yielding the meaning 'cause to be internal'. Because the category changes, we're pretty sure that *-ize* is a derivational suffix. Tense markers for present and past go after the derivational suffix, resulting in *internalizes* and *internalized*. Schematizing the base additions as D for derivational affix and I for inflectional affix, these verbs then have the sequence BASE-D-I. The opposite is clearly ungrammatical: *\*internal-ed-ize*.

## 5.8 Clitics

These are bits of words whose status hovers between words and affixes. Because clitic behavior is complex across languages, clitics are difficult to define succinctly. They are bound forms, unstressed phonologically, correspond to full words and usually quite restricted in where they appear. Although bound, they aren't affixes. Because clitics are a wide topic, only a few rather concrete examples are presented.

A well-known clitic in English is the so-called contraction *n't* used in negating a verb. It's bound and must appear at the end of an auxiliary verb such as *be*, *do* or *have* but never on the verb itself: *She isn't here*; *Don't you think so?*; *I haven't finished the chapter yet*. The full-word correlate is *not*: *She is not here, I have not finished the chapter yet*, although *Do you not think so*? sounds a bit stilted. In any case, *n't* is never a stressed syllable.

The most studied kinds of clitics are pronoun clitics or pronominal clitics. A few, such as *'m* and *'er*, appear in English.

(30a)   Tell'm to get her early!
(30b)   Call'er before you leave!

The *'m* in (30a) is ambiguous, as the full forms are both *him* and *them*. The full form for *Call'er* (sounds exactly like *caller*) is *Call her*.

Other languages make fuller use of pronominal clitics. Most French pronouns, although usually written as independent words, are actually clitics. They aren't stressed, and they immediately precede the verb, as if they are attached like an affix. The pronominal *je*, ('I'), is pronounced as unstressed [ʒə]. When used directly as the subject of the verb, these weak unstressed forms are used. When focused and receiving stress, a nonclitic form *moi* [mwa] must be used.

(31a)  Clitic *je*:            J'irai
                               I'will.go
                               'I'll go'
(31b)  Stressed form *moi*     moi, j'irai   /   *je, j'irai
                               me, I'will.go
                               'Me, I'll go'

If clitics are bound forms, why not just call them affixes? Often, but not always, clitics receive little or no main stress, as is often the case with affixes. Other properties of clitics also overlap with the properties of affixes, too. But two criteria apply fairly consistently in identifying clitics as separate from affixes. One has already been mentioned: clitics have full-word correlates. Corresponding to *'er* is *her*, and corresponding to *'s* in *Dana's late* is *is*, i.e., *Dana is late*. Affixes, however, have no full-word alternative. For example, there's no single word to replace *-ed* in *walked, talked, painted*. Similarly, the possessive clitic, also *'s*, in *Alex's ferret* has no full word to replace it.

The other notable and fairly consistent property of clitics is that, unlike affixes, they can occur with various categories of host words. Affixes such as past *-ed* can go only on verbs not nouns or adjectives or prepositions: **morphology-ed*, **happy-ed*, **about-ed*. The future clitic *'ll*, corresponding to *will*, can follow various categories.

(32)   She'll leave tomorrow.
       That woman'll leave tomorrow.
       That guy who sang'll leave tomorrow.
       The girl who seems absurdly happy'll leave tomorrow.
       The person I gave some money to'll pay me back tomorrow.

Linearly, *'ll* appears to be attaching to various categories: pronoun, noun, verb, adjective and preposition, quite unlike the behavior of affixes. What's really going on is that the clitic attaches to entire phrases and is restricted to a phrase-final position, regardless of the category of the word immediately preceding it. The examples in (33) are identical to those in (32) but with the phrases to which the clitics attach indicated in brackets.

(33)    [She]'ll leave tomorrow
        [That woman]'ll leave tomorrow
        [That guy who sang]'ll leave tomorrow
        [The girl who seems absurdly happy]'ll leave tomorrow
        [The person I gave some money to]'ll pay me back tomorrow.

## 5.9 Summary

This chapter identified derivation as a specific wordformation process for making new lexemes. Derivation is accomplished through affixation, sometimes changing the category of the stem and usually changing meaning. Other derivational phenomena include compounding and incorporation. The later sections of the chapter brought back inflection from Chapter 4 to show the relationship between them in building words and how the two kinds of morphology, derivation and inflection, differ in principled if not absolutely clear ways.

## 5.10 Exercises

1. Following up on the *-ness* suffix discussed in Section 5.2, observe and analyze the following words that end with *-ness* to test the claim that *-ness* suffixes to adjectives. Identify the stems that *–ness* attaches to and what category the stem is. Note whether the stem is simple or complex, and if complex, identify the morphemes in the stem. Comment on any other factors that mitigate a simple analysis in terms of word structure and compositional semantics.

Aggressiveness, appropriateness, attractiveness, awareness, awkwardness, bitterness, blackness, blindness, boldness, brightness, business, cleanliness, closeness, competitiveness, completeness,

connectedness, consciousness, coolness, correctness, craziness, darkness, dizziness, eagerness, effectiveness, emptiness, eyewitness, fair-
ness, fitness, fondness, foolishness, forgiveness, freshness, fullness,
giftedness, goodness, greatness, happiness, hardness, harness, help-
lessness, highness, holiness, homelessness, hopelessness, illness, kind-
ness, laziness, lightness, likeness, loneliness, madness, mindfulness,
nervousness, nothingness, numbness, openness, politeness, prepar-
edness, quickness, randomness, readiness, responsiveness, richness,
righteousness, sadness, sameness, self-awareness, self-consciousness,
selfishness, seriousness, sharpness, shyness, sickness, silliness, soft-
ness, stiffness, stillness, strangeness, sweetness, tenderness, thickness,
toughness, ugliness, unfairness, unhappiness, uniqueness, unwilling-
ness, usefulness, weakness, weariness, wellness, whiteness, wholeness,
wickedness, wilderness, willingness, witness

2. Analyze the following compound nouns, grouped by similar
heads, and comment on their compositionality. That is, discuss the
degree to which you can predict the meaning of the compound based
on the meaning of its parts and the general rule that the modifier precedes the head. To get started, paraphrase the intended meaning as
simply as you can and then expand the paraphrase to more precisely
describe the meanings. Suggest possible alternative meanings.

For example, in the first set (a), the usual meaning of *bookshelf* is 'a
shelf for books' or 'a shelf to put books on', while *steel shelf* denotes
'a shelf made of steel'. Thus, the modifier in *bookshelf* designates
the purpose of the shelf while the modifier in *steel shelf* describes the
material the shelf is made of. These two meanings are perhaps the most
salient, especially in the case of the lexicalized *bookshelf*, but those
meanings are not the only possible ones. Swapping the relationships
of the modifier in the two compounds, *bookshelf* could conceivably
mean 'a shelf made out of books' while *steel shelf* could conceivably
denote 'a shelf for putting steel on'. While the head in all cases does
seem to denote some kind of shelf, the meaning of the modifier and its
semantic relation to the head are variable. Hence, these compounds are
not entirely compositional.

(i)   bookshelf steel shelf
(ii)  tree house doghouse outhouse lighthouse

(iii) highchair Adirondack chair dining room chair committee chair electric chair

(iv) garage sale winter sale towel sale baby sale

## 5.11 Arguable Answers to Exercises

1. Yes, the data confirm that, overwhelmingly, *-ness* suffixes to adjectives to make nouns. The stem is usually simple, and the meaning of the word is largely compositional. So, from the simple adjective stem *dark* we get *darkness*, 'the state of being dark'.

Some of the stems are complex, with at least two morphemes, including: *aggress-ive, attract-ive, clean-ly, fool-ish, home-less, mindful, will-ing*. *Connectedness* is formed with the stem *connected*, the complex perfect participle of the verb *connect*; verbal participles can also function as adjectives, so *-ness* can legitimately attach to these participles.

It's not hard to guess that *business* is related to the adjective *busy*, but *business* is not simply 'the state of being busy'. English also has the more compositionally transparent word *busyness* which DOES mean 'the state of being busy'. Note the differences in spelling and pronunciation between *business* and *busyness*.

It's not clear that *cleanliness* is, as it looks in the spelling, *-ness* suffixed to *cleanly*. By itself, *cleanly* is an adverb, not an adjective. However, while the adverb is pronounced [klinli] the stem of *cleanliness* is [klɛnli], so there's something less than clear compositionally going on.

Although *-ness* usually goes on adjectives, the data do include exceptions, as in some words, *-ness* is going on something other than an adjective. The stem of *forgiveness* seems to be the verb *forgive*, *nothingness* is built on the stem *nothing*, and *likeness* doesn't seem to have an adjectival *like* as its stem. Further, there are a few curve balls in the data in which the *-ness* at the end of the word probably doesn't involve the *-ness* suffix at all: *harness, witness, eyewitness* and *wilderness*. In those cases, removing *-ness* leaves us with the mysterious *harn-, wit-, eyewit-* and *wilder-* (note the difference in pronunciation between this *wilder*, [wɪldər], and the adjective *wilder* 'more wild', pronounced [waildər]). Such words aren't semantically compositional, at least not obviously, although the compositionality may have been more apparent to speakers of historically earlier stages of English. Note that *eyewitness* can be analyzed as a compound of *eye* and *witness*.

Then there are the *self-* examples. Because, as the data attest, *-ness* usually goes on adjectives, and because both *aware* and *self-aware* are adjectives, both can be the stem of the *-ness* suffix. That is, we can conceivably analyze *self-awareness* as [[self-aware] ness] or [self [aware-ness]]. However, a further argument, based on some long-winded grammatical technicalities, is that *self-* is, in some sense, the object of *aware* not of *awareness*. Assuming that's true, then the more arguable structure is [[self-aware] ness], 'the state of being aware of oneself'.

2. There's a lot to say about these compounds, and your discussion may well differ from the following, which is only a sketch of the possible meanings and compositionality and is meant to suggest the kinds of things involved in the question of semantic compositionality in compounds.

The data in (ii) have *house* as the head, although only in *brick house* does it refer to a prototypical house, 'a building in which people live'. And even that definition of the head doesn't rule out condos, apartment buildings, duplexes, etc. *Brick house* most naturally refers to 'house made of bricks', though, of course, wood, metal, plastic, glass and concrete are some other materials commonly used in any house. It's unlikely that any house is made exclusively of bricks; the modifier points only to the salient exterior material. Although not very likely in the real world, *brick house* could do duty as meaning 'a house that bricks live in', on analogy with *doghouse*.

*Tree house*, which, in the right context, could mean 'a house for trees to live in', most naturally is inferred as a locational meaning 'a house in a tree', though it could mean 'a house made of trees'. But more specifically, it means 'a house-like structure built in a tree for children to play in'; certainly, the usual meaning of *tree house* is hardly specified in the simple compound. Like most compounds, *tree house* might get us in the ballpark of the intended meaning, but it isn't strictly compositional.

*Outhouse* refers not to a house per se but to 'a building outside the main house, with a toilet or just a hole in the soil'. It's fair enough to say that *out* does contribute some meaning, but not enough to completely describe what kind of structure an outhouse is. And the head is misleading as well because an outhouse is NOT a house, that is, not a building where people live.

*Lighthouse*, again, is not a house but a specific kind of tall structure, near a body of water, so we have yet another case of *house* not literally meaning 'house'. Given that caveat, *lighthouse* could mean 'a house that's not heavy', or 'a house that makes lights', on analogy with *window factory*, 'a place where windows are manufactured'. But, of course, the standard lexicalized meaning is something like 'a tall structure near a body of water that shines bright light for ships to navigate the coast by' – a lot of information that isn't conveyed in the compound. A more concise, but very incomplete, paraphrase is 'a house that shines light'.

Reiterating the nature of the modifiers and assuming the most natural interpretation of the compounds in (ii), the modifiers refer to a location in *tree house*, purpose in *doghouse*, location and purpose in *outhouse*, purpose in *lighthouse* and material in *brick house*. None of the compounds is completely compositional.

Except for the case of *committee chair*, the other compounds in (iii), in their most natural and lexicalized meanings, do refer to kinds of chairs, things designed to sit on; the *chair* in *committee chair* most naturally refers to a person, the head of some committee. It's possible, though odd and frankly kind of stupid, for *committee chair* to mean 'chair for a committee to sit on'. A highchair is perhaps 'a chair that's high' and is, perhaps, higher than most chairs. However, the height issue is not about the height of the highest point of the back of the chair but, rather, points to the height of the seat. And even so, 'a chair that's high' says nothing about the little people that such a chair is designed for, specifically for eating meals with a detachable tray for containing the food that the little people are eating. This meaning is not particularly compositional. An Adirondack chair, for those who care about naming the myriad designs for chairs, is a chair presumably having something to do with the Adirondack Mountains in upstate New York; the chair was reportedly designed by someone who lived in that area. All good, but when you're shopping for chairs, you probably look for style and function; do you really care about where the chair was originally designed? For *dining room chair*, yes dining room chairs are in the dining room, so *dining room* has a locational and purpose meaning, but it seems that *dining room table chair* might have been more precisely descriptive. Finally, *electric chair* isn't just 'a chair that's electric', and while it is a chair of sorts, its main purpose is obviously not for the comfort of sitting. The modifier *electric*, for the lexicalized meaning of *electric chair*, suggests the means of executing a convicted criminal. But the relationship of the modifier to the head noun *chair* is quite different from the relationship in *electric motor* and *electric eel*, for example.

Finally, the compound nouns in (iv) are particularly revealing about the meaning of the head and the modifiers' semantic relation to the head. *Sale* is harder to define than you might think. A meaning that might come most immediately to mind is 'selling, the act of selling, especially at a discounted price', but that's not quite right for these examples. A towel sale most obviously refers to the availability for purchase rather than the selling itself, which, in any case, might not occur: a towel sale might be a complete flop for a retailer if no customers show up to buy the towels, but it's still a towel sale.

*Garage sale* supposedly take place in someone's garage, so, here, *garage* is a locational description. It could also be 'a sale of garages'. *Winter* in *winter sale* indicates time, not place. *Towel* in *towel sale* is akin to an argument, the thing being sold. On analogy with *towel sale*, *baby sale* could mean 'availability of babies for purchase', but, of course, that's not what *baby sale* usually means. Another meaning is 'a sale operated by babies', akin to 'a company sale (of the whole or part of the company)'. In fact, the relationship of *baby* to *sale* is quite indirect: 'the availability for purchase of stuff for babies'. *Baby* not the goal of the sale but of the kind of stuff that's being sold.

Summing up, assuming a clear enough reference for the heads of compounds, the relationship of the modifier to the head is never unambiguous, as various relationships, such as time, place, material, location, purpose, etc., are available. Many meanings are filtered out of the compound if the compound is lexicalized and common, but other meanings are usually available even if not very likely. The description intended by the modifier may narrow down the denotation of the head, but, strictly speaking, the meanings of the whole compound are not particularly compositional.

# Chapter 6

# Final Comments

Morphology is that part of the grammar that accounts for wordformation in a language. The word morphology also refers to the scientific
study of wordformation in languages, a subfield of linguistics.

At the bottom of a speaker's word-making capacity is their large
lexicon, the network of morphemes, minimal sound-meaning pairs in
spoken languages or visual sign-meaning pairs in sign languages. The
speaker also has access to an internalized set of grammatical rules for
assembling words with morphological structure. The lexicon and the
word-making rules interact with other parts of the grammar: syntax,
phonology and semantics.

There are two main kinds of wordformation. Inflection accounts for
all the related wordforms in a lexeme (e.g., *walk*, *walks*, *walked*, *walk-*
*ing*); derivation creates new lexemes (e.g., *walker*, *sidewalk*, *walkie-*
*talkie*). Both inflection and derivation may apply within the same
word, and resulting words, depending on the language and the particular construction, can become quite long. There is some degree of
compositionality in wordformation in that if the morphemes are known
and the rules for putting them together are known, the meaning of the
whole word can be deduced. However, a lot of wordformation, especially derivation, results in meanings that are far from compositional.

The basic picture, however, is deviled by details. Perhaps the most
glaring problem is that a whole field of study is dedicated to the making of words, when linguists lack a rock-solid definition or understanding of what exactly a word is. No definition fits all the expressions we

think are words in a language, let alone the expressions that purport-edly pass for words across languages. How do we know those long Crow words in Chapter 5 are really words? We don't. If they have all, most or some of the properties attributed to wordhood, then we say they're words. If we rely on phonological criteria, such as the number of stressed syllables and which syllable(s) are stressed, some expres-sions pass for words, although other morphological criteria might not be so clear-cut. But that may simply indicate that phonological words don't correspond exactly to morphological words.

There are at least two ways to proceed from the impasse. One is to assume that we've been barking up some of the wrong trees and that more precise identification of word criteria and more comprehensive definitions of wordhood will follow with ongoing research. It may turn out that wordhood is a fluid thing, a more-or-less phenomenon, within and across languages, and that there is no clean division between things that are words (by some definition) and other kinds of expres-sions in the language. Of course, let's remember that the difficulty in finding a universal definition of what a word is doesn't mean a defini-tion doesn't exist.

Related to the issue of wordhood is the fact that most, if not all, of the categories relevant to morphology are also plagued with non-discreteness. Categorizing nouns and verbs, compounds and phrases, derivation and inflection, clitics and affixes, pronominal clitics and personal pronouns faces the same lack of unambiguous criteria for dis-tinguishing one class of items from another.

All these technical problems are part of the fascination morpholo-gists have with wordformation. Working with an assumption that words do exist and that they're formed in certain structural patterns and that some of these patterns are the crosslinguistically preferred ways of making words, morphologists work to understand not only the words that are attested in use and listed in dictionaries but also the human capacity for creating new words, sometimes with conscious deliberate planning, as in giving a new product a catchy name for mar-keting, and most of the time without conscious intent, just letting the morphological part of the grammar do its thing – form words.

*The Study of Words: An Introduction* has presented some of the fundamental things morphologists think they know about words and what the fundamental questions are. The book covered the basic topics and the kinds of data that morphologists want to understand. Some theory has been introduced, but I've avoided sinking too deeply into various schools of thought about wordformation and the many arcane subtleties about morphology – subtleties that are the bread and butter of linguists who devote their careers to morphology but that would unnecessarily hinder a basic introduction to the field.

The book started with *antidisestablishmentarianism*, which is not the longest word in English but long and complex enough to make for interesting dissection. Though long, it's probably a single word; it's certainly not a prepositional phrase or sentence. Granted, it's probably a consciously and artificially long word, but it *IS* a word, legitimately constructed with some morphemes from the lexicon and the appending of a bunch of affixes. Speakers' knowledge of morphology, picked up through the process of mostly untutored language acquisition in the first years of life, allows for them to break this not-very-useful word into its constituent morphemes and understand, sort of, why *antidisestablishmentarianism* means what it means.

# Bibliography

Abney, Steven. 1987. The English noun phrase in its sentential aspect. MIT PhD Dissertation. Available at http://www.vinartus.com/spa/87a.pdf.

Aitchison, Jean. 2012. *Words in the Mind: An Introduction to the Mental Lexicon*, 4th edition. Malden: John Wiley & Sons.

Allen, W. Sidney. 1956. Structure and system in the Abaza verbal complex. *Transactions of the Philological Society* 1956: 127–276.

American Chemical Society. n.d. Chemistry is everywhere. https://www.acs.org/content/acs/en/education/whatischemistry/everywhere.html. Retrieved on 2021-01-01.

*American Heritage Dictionary of the English Language*, 3rd edition. 1992. Boston: Houghton Mifflin.

Anderson, Stephen R. 1992. *A-Morphous Morphology*. Cambridge: Cambridge University Press.

Aronoff, Mark. 1976. *Word Formation in Generative Grammar*. Cambridge: Cambridge University Press.

Audring, Jenny and Masini, Francesca. 2019. Introduction: Theory and theories in morphology. In Jenny Audring and Francesca Masini (eds.), *The Oxford Handbook of Morphological Theory*, 1–8. Oxford: Oxford University Press.

Baker, Mark. 1988. *Incorporation: A Theory of Grammatical Function Changing*. Chicago and London: University of Chicago Press.

Baker, Mark. 2001. *The Atoms of Language*. New York: Basic Books.

Baker, Mark. 2003. *Lexical Categories: Verbs, Nouns, and Adjectives*. Cambridge: Cambridge University Press.

Barnes, Janet. 1984. Evidentials in the Tuyuca verb. *International Journal of American Linguistics* 50(3): 255–271.

Barrett, Martyn. 1995. Early lexical development. In Paul Fletcher and Brian MacWhinney (eds.), *The Handbook of Child Language*, 362–392. Oxford: Blackwell Publishers Ltd.

Bauer, Laurie. 1983. *English Word-Formation*. Cambridge: Cambridge University Press.

Bauer, Laurie. 1988. *Introducing Linguistic Morphology*. Edinburgh: Edinburgh University Press.

Bauer, Laurie. 2017. *Compounds and Compounding*. Cambridge: Cambridge University Press.

Bauer, Laurie, Lieber, Rochelle and Plag, Ingo. 2013. *The Oxford Reference Guide to English Morphology*. Oxford: Oxford University Press.

Beard, Robert. 1998. Derivation. In Andrew Spencer and Arnold M. Zwicky (eds.), *The Handbook of Morphology*, 44–65. Oxford: Blackwell.

Berlin, Brent and Kay, Paul. 1969. *Basic Color Terms*. Berkeley: University of California Press.

Blevins, Juliette. 2012. Infixation. CUNY Graduate Center. August 29, 2012. Available at https://julietteblevins.ws.gc.cuny.edu/files/2016/10/Blevins2012_Infixationrev1.pdf.

Blevins, Juliette. 2014. Infixation. In Rochelle Lieber and Pavol Štekauer (eds.), *The Oxford Handbook of Derivational Morphology*, 136–151. Oxford: Oxford University Press.

Bloom, Paul. 2000. *How Children Learn the Meanings of Words*. Cambridge: Bradford/MIT Press.

Booij, Geert E. 2009. Morphological analysis. In Bernd Heine and Heiko Narrog (eds.), *The Oxford Handbook of Linguistic Analysis*, 507–529. Oxford: Oxford University Press.

Booij, Geert. 2010. Morphological analysis. In Bernd Heine and Heiko Narrog (eds.), *The Oxford Handbook of Linguistic Analysis*. Oxford: Oxford University Press. Available at https://www.academia.edu/24145648/Morphological_Analysis?email_work_card=view-paper. Retrieved on 2021-06-12.

Branch, Michael. 1990. Finnish. In Bernard Comrie (ed.), *The World's Major Languages*, 593–617. New York and Oxford: Oxford University Press.

Brysbaert, Marc, Stevens, Michaël, Mandera, Paweł and Keuleers, Emmanuel. 2016. How many words do we know? Practical estimates of vacabulary size dependent on word definition, the degree of language input and participant's age. *Frontiers in Psychology*. July 29, 2016. Available at https://www.frontiersin.org/articles/10.3389/fpsyg.2016.01116/full. Retrieved on 2021-07-05.

Carstairs-McCarthy, Andrew. 2018. *An Introduction to English Morphology: Words and Their Structure*. Edinburgh: Edinburgh University Press.

Chomsky, Noam. 1986. *Knowledge of Language*. New York: Praeger.

Clark, Eve. 1995. Later lexical development and word formation. In Paul Fletcher and Brian MacWhinney (eds.), *The Handbook of Child Language*, 393–412. Oxford: Blackwell Publishers Ltd.

Corbett, Greville. 2000. *Number*. Cambridge: Cambridge University Press.

Croft, William. 1990. *Typology and Universals*. Cambridge: Cambridge University Press.

Croft, William. 2000. Parts of speech as language universals and as language-particular categories. In Petra M. Vogel and Bernard Comrie (eds.), *Approaches to the Typology of Word Classes*, 65–102. Berlin: Mouton de Gruyter.

Crowley, Terry and Bowern, Claire. 2010. *An Introduction to Historical Linguistics*, 4th edition. Oxford: Oxford University Press.

Cysouw, Michael. 2013. Inclusive/Exclusive distinction in independent pronouns. In Matthew S. Dryer and Martin Haspelmath (eds.), *The World Atlas of Language Structures Online*. Leipzig: Max Planck Institute for Evolutionary Anthropology. Available at http://wals.info/chapter/39. Retrieved on 2021-07-09.

Davies, William. 1986. *Choctaw Verb Agreement and Universal Grammar*. Dordrecht: Reidel.

de Haan, Ferdinande. 2013. Coding of evidentiality. In Matthew S. Dryer and Martin Haspelmath (eds.), *The World Atlas of Language Structures Online*. Leipzig: Max Planck Institute for Evolutionary Anthropology. Available at http://wals.info/chapter/78. Retrieved on 2021-07-08.

Derbyshire, Desmond C. 1979. *Hixkaryana*. Amsterdam: North Holland Publishing.

Diessel, Holger. 1999. *Demonstratives: Form, Function and Grammaticalization*. Amsterdam: John Benjamins.

Diessel, Holger. 2013. Distance contrasts in demonstratives. In Matthew S. Dryer and Martin Haspelmath (eds.), *The World Atlas of Language Structures Online*. Leipzig: Max Planck Institute for Evolutionary Anthropology. Available at http://wals.info/chapter/41. Retrieved on 2021-07-10.

Dixon, R.M.W. 2014. *Making New Words: Morphological Derivation in English*. Oxford: Oxford University Press.

Dorvlo, K. 2008. *A Grammar of Logba (Ikpana)*. Utrecht: LOT.

Dryer, Matthew S. 2013a. Prefixing vs. suffixing in inflectional morphology. In Matthew S. Dryer and Martin Haspelmath (eds.), *The World Atlas of Language Structures Online*. Leipzig: Max Planck Institute for Evolutionary Anthropology. Available at http://wals.info/chapter/26. Retrieved 2021-07-08.

Dryer, Matthew S. 2013b. Position of case affixes. In Matthew S. Dryer and Martin Haspelmath (eds.), *The World Atlas of Language Structures Online*. Leipzig: Max Planck Institute for Evolutionary Anthropology. Available at http://wals.info/chapter/51. Retrieved on 2021-07-08.

Dryer, Matthew S. 2013c. Position of tense-aspect affixes. In Matthew S. Dryer and Martin Haspelmath (eds.), *The World Atlas of Language Structures Online*. Leipzig: Max Planck Institute for Evolutionary Anthropology. Available at http://wals.info/chapter/69. Retrieved on 2021-07-08.

Dryer, Matthew S. 2013d. Coding of nominal plurality. In Matthew S. Dryer and Martin Haspelmath (eds.), *The World Atlas of Language Structures Online*. Leipzig: Max Planck Institute for Evolutionary Anthropology. Available at http://wals.info/chapter/33. Retrieved on 2021-07-08.

Dryer, Matthew S. 2013e. Definite articles. In Matthew S. Dryer and Martin Haspelmath (eds.), *The World Atlas of Language Structures Online*. Leipzig: Max Planck Institute for Evolutionary Anthropology. Available at http://wals.info/chapter/37. Retrieved on 2021-07-09.

Dryer, Matthew S. 2013f. Indefinite articles. In Matthew S. Dryer and Martin Haspelmath (eds.), *The World Atlas of Language Structures Online*. Leipzig: Max Planck Institute for Evolutionary Anthropology. Available at http://wals.info/chapter/38. Retrieved on 2021-07-10.

Dryer, Matthew S. and Haspelmath, Martin (eds.). 2013. *The World Atlas of Language Structures Online*. Leipzig: Max Planck Institute for Evolutionary Anthropology.

Efron, Bradley and Thisted, Ronald. 1976. Estimating the number of unseen species: How many words did Shakespeare Know? *Biometrika* 63(3): 435–447. https://doi.org/10.2307/2335721.

Eichenwald, Kurt. 2005. *Conspiracy of Fools: A True Story*. New York: Broadway Books.

Fenson, L., Dale, P.S., Reznick, J.S., Thal, D., Bates, E., Hartung, J., Pethick, S. and Reilly, J. 1993. *The MacArthur Communicative Development Inventories: User's Guide and Technical Manual*. San Deigo. Singular Publishing Group.

Freidin, Robert. 2012. *Syntax: Basic Concepts and Applications*. Cambridge: Cambridge University Press.

Fromkin, Victoria, Rodman, Robert and Hyams, Mina. 2014. *An Introduction to Language*, 10th edition. Boston: Wadsworth.

Garcia Marquez, Gabriel. 1970. *One Hundred Years of Solitude (English Translation)*. New York: Harper & Row. Originally published in Spanish in 1967.

Gardani, Francesco. 2018. On morphological borrowing. *Language and Linguistics Compass* 12(10): 1–17.

Gender Neutral Pronouns. n.d. https://forge-forward.org/wp-content/uploads/2020/08/gender-neutral-pronouns1.pdf. Retrieved on 2021-05-01.

Gibson, Ted and Conway, Bevil R. 2017. The world has millions of colors. Why do we only name a few? The conversation: Smithsonian .com. September 19, 2017. Available at https://www.smithsonianmag .com/science-nature/why-different-languages-name-different-colors -180964945/#2QqV82uLcZ4oTgoq.03.

Gil, David. 2013. Numeral classifiers. In Matthew S. Dryer and Martin Haspelmath (eds.), *The World Atlas of Language Structures Online*. Leipzig: Max Planck Institute for Evolutionary Anthropology. Available at http://wals.info/chapter/55. Retrieved on 2021-07-09.

Gleason, H.A. 1961. *An Introduction to Descriptive Linguistics*. New York: Holt, Rinehart and Winston.

Golston, Chris, Boyle, John and Gebhardt, Lewis. Crow has no incorporation. Submitted manuscript.

Goudswaard, N. 2005. *The Begak (Ida'an) Language of Sabah*. Utrecht: LOT.

Graczyk, Randolph. 2007. *A Grammar of Crow*. Lincoln and London: University of Nebraska Press.

Halle, Morris and Marantz, Alec. 1993. Distributed morphology and the piece of inflection. In Kenneth Hale and Samuel Keyser (eds.), *The View From Building 20: Essays in Linguistics in Honor of Sylvain Brombeger*, 111–176. Cambridge: MIT Press.

Hambly, Matt. What is chemistry? NewScientist Ltd. https://www.newscientist .com/definition/chemistry/. Retrieved on 2020-04-14.

Hardy, Thomas. 1960. *Far From the Madding Crowd*. New York: Signet Classics. Original work published in 1874.

Harley, Heidi and Noyer, Rolf. 1999. Distributed morphology. *Glot International* 4(4): 3–9.

Haspelmath, Martin and Sims, Andrea D. 2010. *Understanding Morphology*, 2nd edition. London: Hodder Education.

Haugen, Einar. 1990. Danish, Norwegian and Swedish. In Bernard Comrie (ed.), *The World's Major Languages*, 157–179. New York and Oxford: Oxford University Press.

Hudak, Thomas John. 1990. Thai. In Bernard Comrie (ed.), *The World's Major Languages*, 757–775. New York and Oxford: Oxford University Press.

Hutchison, John P. 1981. *The Kanuri Language: A Reference Grammar*. Madison: University of Wisconsin African Studies Program.

Hyman, Larry. 2000. Suprasegmental units. In Geert Booij, Christian Lehmann and Joachim Mugdan (eds.), *Morphology - A Handbook on Inflection and Word Formation*, Volume I. Berlin: De Gruyter.

Iggesen, Oliver, A. 2013. Number of Cases. In Matthew S. Dryer and Martin Haspelmath (eds.), *The World Atlas of Language Structures Online*. Leipzig: Max Planck Institute for Evolutionary Anthropology. Available at http://wals.info/chapter/49. Accessed on 2021-11-02.

Indo-European Languages. https://en.wikipedia.org/wiki/Indo-European _languages. Retrieved on 2021-09-20.

Ingham, Bruce. 2003. *Lakota*. Muenchen: Lincom Europa.

Inkelas, Sharon. 2014. The interaction between morphology and phonology. In John A. Goldsmith, Jason Riggle and Alan C. L. Yu (eds.), *The Handbook of Morphological Theory*, 2nd edition, 68–102. Malden: Wiley Blackwell.

Inkelas, Sharon and Orgun, C. Orhan. 1998. Level (non)ordering in recursive morphology: Evidence from Turkish. In Steven Lapointe, Diane Brentari and Patrick Farrell (eds.), *Morphology and Its Relation to Phonology and Syntax*, 360–410. Stanford: CSLI.

International Phonetic Association. https://www.internationalphoneticas sociation.org/content/full-ipa-chart. Retrieved on 2021-05-03.

IPA Chart with Sounds. 2021. International. PhoneticAlphabet.org. Retrieved on 2021-05-03.

Jackendoff, Ray. 2002. *Foundations of Language: Brain, Meaning, Grammar, Evolution*. Oxford: Oxford University Press.

Kaye, Alan S. 1990. Arabic. In Bernard Comrie (ed.), *The World's Major Languages*, 664–685. New York and Oxford: Oxford University Press.

Kornfilt, Jaklin. 1987. Turkish and the Turkic languages. In Bernard Comrie (ed.), *The World's Major Languages*, 619–644. New York and Oxford: Oxford University Press.

Kornfilt, Jaklin. 1997. *Turkish*. London: Routledge.

Koshevoy, Alexey. 2018. *Morphological causatives in Abaza*. Basic Research Program Working Papers Series: Linguistics. Moscow: National Research University Higher School of Economics. Available at https://wp.hse.ru/ data/2018/12/25/1143086542/75LNG2018.pdf.

Language Family. https://en.wikipedia.org/wiki/Language_family. Accessed September 21, 2021.

Lewis, G.I. 1967. *Turkish Grammar*. Oxford: Clarendon Press.

Lichtenberk, Frantisek. 1983. *A Grammar of Manam*. Oceanic Linguistics Special Publications, no. 18. Honolulu: University of Hawaii Press.

Lieber, Rochelle. 2016. *Introducing Morphology*, 2nd edition. Cambridge: Cambridge University Press.

List of Dictionaries by Number of Words. Wikipedia. https://en.wikipedia
.org/wiki/List_of_dictionaries_by_number_of_words#:~:text=Oxford
%20Dictionary%20has%20273%2C000%20headwords,derivative
%20words%20included%20as%20subentries. Retrieved on 2021-04-10.

Lvovin, Anatole V. 1997. *An Introduction to Languages of the World*. New
York: Oxford University Press.

Lynch, Jack. 2009. *The Lexicographer's Dilemma*. New York: Walker & Co.

Lyons, Christopher. 1999. *Definiteness*. Cambridge: Cambridge University
Press.

Mahootian, Shahrzad. 1997. *Persian*. London: Routledge.

Mallory, J.P. 1989. *In Search of the Indo-Europeans: Language, Archaeology
and Myth*. London: Thames and Hudson.

Marchand, Hans. 1966. *The Categories and Types of Present-Day English
Word-Formation: A Synchronic-Diachronic Approach*. Tuscaloosa:
University of Alabama Press.

McCarthy, John. 1979. Formal problems in semitic phonology and morphology.
MIT doctoral dissertation.

McCarthy, John. 1981. A prosodic theory of nonconcatenative native
morphology. *Linguistic Inquiry* 12: 373–418.

McLean, Bethany and Elkind, Peter. 2003. *The Smartest Guys in the Room: The
Amazing Rise and Scandalous Fall of Enron*. New York: Penguin Books.

McWhorter, John. 2011. *What Language Is (and What It Isn't and What It
Could Be)*. New York: Gotham Books.

Mondloch, James L. 1978. *Basic Quiche Grammar*. Albany: Institute for
Mesoamerican Studies.

Moravcsik, Edith A. 2013. *Introducing Language Typology*. Cambridge:
Cambridge University Press.

Most Common Words in English. https://en.wikipedia.org/wiki/Most_
common_words_in_English. Retrieved on 2021-03-01.

Murdoch, James L. 1978. *Basic Quiche Grammar*. Albany: Institute for
Mesoamerican Studies.

Nagy, Gregory. 2017. The documentation of Greek. In Jared Klein, Brian
Joseph and Matthias Fritz (eds.), *Handbook of Comparative and Historical
Indo-European Linguistics*, 625–637. Berlin and Boston: Walter de
Gruyter.

O'Grady, William, Archibald, John, Aronoff, Mark and Rees-Miller, Janie.
2010. *Contemporary Linguistics: An Introduction*, 6th edition. Boston:
Bedford/St. Martins.

Östen, Dahl and Velupillai, Viveka. 2013a. The past tense. In Matthew S. Dryer
and Martin Haspelmath (eds.), *The World Atlas of Language Structures*

*Online*. Leipzig: Max Planck Institute for Evolutionary Anthropology. Available at http://wals.info/chapter/66. Retrieved on 2021-11-02.

Östen, Dahl and Velupillai, Viveka. 2013b. Perfective/imperfective aspect. In Matthew S. Dryer and Martin Haspelmath (eds.), *The World Atlas of Language Structures Online*. Leipzig: Max Planck Institute for Evolutionary Anthropology. Available at http://wals.info/chapter/65. Retrieved on 2021-11-02.

Over the Rainbow. n.d. https://genius.com/Judy-garland-over-the-rainbow-lyrics. Retrieved on 2021-05-06.

Palmer, P.R. 1986. *Mood and Modality: Cambridge Textbooks in Linguistics*. Cambridge: Cambridge University Press.

Parkinson, Stephen. 1990. Portuguese. In Bernard Comrie (ed.), *The World's Major Languages*, 260–278. New York and Oxford: Oxford University Press.

Payne, Thomas E. 1997. *Describing Morphosyntax*. Cambridge: Cambridge University Press.

Plank, Frans. 1999. Split morphology: How agglutination and flexion mix. *Linguistic Typology* 3(3): 279–340.

Progovac, Ljiljana. 2015. *Evolutionary Syntax*. Oxford: Oxford University Press.

Pustejovsky, James and Batiulova, Olga. 2019. *The Lexicon*. Cambridge: Cambridge University Press.

*Random House Dictionary of the English Language*, 2nd edition. 1987. New York: Random House Inc.

Rijkhoff, Jan. 2000. When can a language have adjectives? An implicational universal. In Petra M. Vogel and Bernard Comrie (eds.), *Approaches to the Typology of Word Classes*, 217–258. Berlin: Mouton de Gruyter.

Rood, David S. 1976. *Wichita Grammar*. New York and London: Garland Publishing Inc.

Samavati, Fatemeh. 2022. Direct object case marker in modern Persian. California State University Fresno Master's Thesis.

Siewierska, Anna. 2013. Gender distinctions in independent personal pronouns. In Matthew S. Dryer and Martin Haspelmath (eds.), *The World Atlas of Language Structures Online*. Leipzig: Max Planck Institute for Evolutionary Anthropology. Available at http://wals.info/chapter/44. Retrieved on 2021-07-09.

Sloat, Clarence and Taylor, Sharon. 1992. *The Structure of English Words*. Dubuque: Kendall/Hunt.

Spence, Melanie J. and Freeman, Mark S. 1996. Newborn infants prefer the maternal low-pass filtered voice, but not the maternal whispered voice. *Infant Behavior and Development* 109: 199–212.

Stone, Gerald. 1990. Polish. In Bernard Comrie (ed.), *The World's Major Languages*, 348–366. New York and Oxford: Oxford University Press.

Stump, Gregory T. 1998. Inflection. In Andrew Spencer and Arnold M. Zwicky (eds.), *The Handbook of Morphology*, 13–43. Oxford: Blackwell.

Spencer, Andrew. 1991. *Morphological Theory*. Malden: Blackwell.

Suchada, G. 2004. Plang grammar as spoken in Huay Namkhun Village, Chang Rai Province. Mahidol University MA thesis.

Terrill, A. 1999. A grammar of Lavukaleve. A Papuan language of the Solomon Islands. PhD dissertation. Australian National University.

Topping, Donald M. 1973. *Chamorro Reference Grammar*. Honolulu: University Press of Hawaii.

*Urban Dictionary*. https://www.urbandictionary.com/. Retrieved on 2021-04-01.

Velupillai, Viveka. 2012. *An Introduction to Linguistic Typology*. Amsterdam: John Benjamins.

Wallace, Karen Kay. 1993. Verb incorporation and agreement in crow. UCLA PhD dissertation.

Whaley, Lindsay J. 1997. *Introduction to Typology*. Thousand Oaks: Sage Publications.

Windfuhr, Gernot L. 1990. Persian. In Bernard Comrie (ed.), *The World's Major Languages*, 523–546. New York and Oxford: Oxford University Press.

Wootton, David. 2015. *The Invention of Science: A New History of the Scientific Revolution*. New York: HarperCollins.

# Index

For Product Safety Concerns and Information please contact our EU
representative GPSR@taylorandfrancis.com
Taylor & Francis Verlag GmbH, Kaufingerstraße 24, 80331 München, Germany

www.ingramcontent.com/pod-product-compliance
Ingram Content Group UK Ltd.
Pitfield, Milton Keynes, MK11 3LW, UK
UKHW021446080625
459435UK00012B/381